AT THE GRAVE O]

AT THE GRAVE OF CIVILIZATION?

A Spiritual Approach to Popular Culture

Sevak Gulbekian

TEMPLE LODGE
London

To Sergei O. Prokofieff

Temple Lodge Publishing
51 Queen Caroline Street
London W6 9QL

Published by Temple Lodge 1996

First published in book form in German translation under the title
Wetterleuchten im Zeitgeschehen by Verlag am Goetheanum, Dornach,
Switzerland, 1995. A number of the essays have been published
previously in English in earlier versions (see Notes section for details)

A catalogue record for this book is available from the British Library

ISBN 0 904693 78 3

Cover illustration by Andrew Morgan, based on a section of the
'red window' in the Goetheanum, Switzerland
Design by Studio MAOSS
Typeset by DP Photosetting, Aylesbury, Bucks.
Printed and bound in Great Britain by Cromwell Press Limited,
Broughton Gifford, Wiltshire

'... And in the course of the twentieth century, when the first century after Kali-Yuga has elapsed, humanity will either stand at the grave of all civilization or at the beginning of the epoch when Michael's battle on behalf of his impulse will be fought out in the souls of those people who in their hearts have united reason with spirituality.'

Rudolf Steiner, 19 July 1924

'Anthroposophy does not exist to send people off to sleep, but to make them really wide awake. We are living at a time when it is necessary for people to wake up.'

Rudolf Steiner, 13 October 1917

CONTENTS

FOREWORD ix

1 THE STRUGGLE FOR THE CONSCIOUSNESS
 SOUL
 The Priest Who Didn't Believe in God 1
 The Nun and the Comet 4

2 BEAVIS AND BUTT-HEAD
 The Ahrimanization of the Consciousness Soul 8

3 FILMS, VIOLENCE AND 'REALITY' IN ART 18

4 GANGSTA RAP, REALITY AND
 'SUPER-MATERIALISM' 30

5 THE CASE OF DAVID ICKE
 Modern Manifestations of Evil 46

6 THE QUESTION OF RACE, I
 Malcolm X and the Michael Impulse 59

7 THE QUESTION OF RACE, II
 A Spiritual Perspective 78

APPENDIX: READING THE SIGNS OF THE TIMES
Anthroposophy and Contemporary Culture 92

NOTES AND REFERENCES 104

FOREWORD

The title of this book is extracted from a quotation by Rudolf Steiner (given in full on page v). His words—which refer very directly to our time—convey a picture of humanity standing at a crossroads in its evolution. As we approach the end of the second millennium, Steiner suggests, two possibilities exist: either culture will thoroughly be transformed through a connection with the leading spiritual impulse of our age, or humanity will find itself staring at the grave of civilization.

When Rudolf Steiner founded Anthroposophy (a wisdom of the human being) in the early part of this century, his intention was not to create a new sect or cult—of which we have hundreds today, some highly dangerous—but to initiate a new striving for spiritual truth which, with its detailed methodology and empirical, experiential basis (as opposed to simple faith or belief) was in the tradition of the scientific thinking of his time. In this sense he described Anthroposophy as a *science* of the spirit. And thus he strove—in the face of the profound materialism of the time—to communicate his knowledge of the spirit not through a vague mysticism, but in a form that could be understood with clear human thought.

As we approach the end of this troubled century, materialism—which now permeates every aspect of culture, from economics to religion—is more entrenched and intense than ever. In many ways we can experience that we exist within a culture that is dying, and the fading traditions and certainties of the past seem to suggest that a new impetus is needed to nudge our development forwards. But the regenerated culture that is required should, according to Rudolf Steiner, be based on the spiritual reality which humankind has forgotten throughout the long years of spiritual darkness (known in occultism as Kali-Yuga). Today, therefore, the task of perceiving the existence of the spiritual world—to complement our intricate knowledge of the physical—is more urgent than ever before.

These essays are an attempt to discern occult forces working in contemporary culture. The author does not claim to be clairvoyant or even highly trained in spiritual-scientific methods, and accepts that he may have made errors and misjudgements. Nevertheless, these studies comprise at least an *attempt* to awaken to the spiritual in everyday life.

Throughout the text revisions and additions have been made to the original articles (mostly published elsewhere in earlier versions). Inevitably, though—from the point of view of being immediately contemporary—the outer references and facts will begin to date. However, it is hoped that the studies themselves will remain relevant as the intention has been to demonstrate a particular spiritual approach to reading and comprehending 'the signs of the times'. More can be found about this method from an esoteric perspective in the Appendix.

It should be mentioned that the articles which make up this book were originally composed for a readership conversant with Anthroposophy, and thus occasionally presume a knowledge of certain basic concepts deriving from Rudolf Steiner's spiritual research: for example, higher bodies of the human being which are in the process of development (the intellectual soul and the consciousness soul), and the dual nature of evil (as represented by the spiritual powers of Lucifer and Ahriman). Nevertheless, the general reader should find most of the content comprehensible.

Finally, I would like to thank my Swiss publisher, Joseph

Morel of Verlag am Goetheanum, for taking the original initiative to collect together these essays in a single volume.

Sevak Gulbekian
December 1995

1
THE STRUGGLE FOR THE CONSCIOUSNESS SOUL

The Priest Who Didn't Believe in God

In the last week of July 1994, Anthony Freeman, the priest-in-charge of a picturesque church in the small village of Staplefield in Sussex, England, was sacked from his position by the Bishop of Chichester for 'not believing in God'. A year previously the renegade priest had lost his position as director of post-ordination training, following the publication of his book *God With Us*. The further dismissal caused a letter of protest to be written by 65 Church of England clerics to *The Independent*. In the letter, printed on 28 July, only some of the clerics shared Freeman's views, but all defended his right to freedom of expression within the Church.

In his own words, Anthony Freeman stands for 'a new, bracing beliefless Christianity'. In his book he further declares: 'There is nothing out there—or if there is, we can have no knowledge of it.' In an interview published in his parish magazine, however, he took a slightly different tack when asked if he believed in God. 'Yes,' he replied, 'and to work out what that means is my life's work.' He elaborated further on an ITN news report, saying: 'I believe that when we use the word God we are using it to focus all that's best and highest in our own human hopes and aspirations and ideas.'[1]

As witnessed by the above quotations, the truth of this strange story has philosophical subtleties (which were predictably ignored or trivialized by the popular press). Furthermore—as the letter by the 65 clergymen to *The*

Independent demonstrated—Freeman by no means stands alone in his views. On the contrary, he represents a school of thought within the Church of England, and Christianity as a whole, which seeks to intertwine a humanist philosophy (i.e. a benevolent agnosticism, which teaches that people should love one another, etc.) with a materialistic interpretation of the Gospels and Christianity. Such a philosophy usually reveres 'Jesus the man' as a great teacher of social values and an example of right living, but generally dismisses the cosmic or spiritual aspect of Christianity. In holding such views, Freeman and his fellow 'disbelievers' personify a materialistic stream of thought within theology that is by no means unique or new. (A contemporary example of such theology is the academic Don Cupitt's book *Taking Leave from God*. But even Rudolf Steiner pointed to such tendencies within Christianity during his time, for example in his lectures *From Jesus to Christ* where he uses the term 'Jesuitism' when referring to teachings that centre on 'Jesus' as opposed to 'Christ'.) Despite all this, it is nevertheless somewhat surprising that a *priest* should publicly represent such opinions—particularly as in Church tradition the priest is regarded as being the mediator between man and a spiritual God. One can therefore understand the actions of the Church authorities in the case of Staplefield's extraordinary priest.

Defending his decision, the Bishop of Chichester was forthright about the extent to which internal debate of this kind could be accepted within the Church, stating: 'The whole thing is ridiculous, there must be some limits to what the Church of England will tolerate if it is going to stand for anything at all.' But not all the people of Staplefield agreed with him. Interviewed in *The Independent*, a 19-year-old girl exclaimed: 'He [Freeman] is more in touch with what people think than the bishops are. They're all hypocrites and they were wrong to sack him. He's just being brave enough to ask the questions we all ask.' A 49-year-old woman added: 'He tries to preach how he feels, and he doesn't believe in the resurrection or the virgin birth. He is a good priest and we want him to stay...'[2]

In the context of the widespread materialism of our times episodes of this kind are not to be unexpected. But our approach to understanding such phenomena through spiritual science would be one-dimensional if we were merely to dismiss Freeman for his lack of concepts regarding the spiritual world. Of course, we can draw the conclusion that events such as these indicate the need, perhaps more than ever before, for a clear spiritual-scientific knowledge of the world and humanity, as we find in Anthroposophy. We can also note that Freeman's statement that 'we can have no knowledge of it [the spiritual world]' is in direct contradiction to all that was achieved in the field of spiritual science by Rudolf Steiner. However, if we consider the case of Anthony Freeman from another point of view, it takes on a new value. For within his inner struggle to understand Christianity we are provided with a picture of the individual spirit—the personal conscience—in its search for knowledge that is based on direct experience. Opposed to this personal exploration stand the old established spiritual forms of the past—as portrayed in this instance by the Church—with their dogmas, creeds and certainties.

In his book *Theosophy* Rudolf Steiner characterized the consciousness soul as that eternal part of the individuality which carries within itself 'truth and goodness'. Freeman's fight for individual truth led him to materially-bound conclusions, away from an acknowledgement of the spiritual world in all its multifaceted reality. But the process of his personal quest for knowledge is one we can respect deeply as modern human beings, for we recognize within it the striving of the consciousness soul.

As one of his parishioners so eloquently expressed: 'He's just brave enough to ask the questions we all ask.'

The Nun and the Comet

As the last fragments of the comet 'Shoemaker-Levy 9' crashed into the planet Jupiter during July 1994, the London-based Catholic nun, prophetess, and self-styled 'astronomer' Sofia Richmond must have experienced ambivalent feelings. Richmond, who is also known as Sister Marie Gabriel and Sophie Segatis Paprocki Orvid Puciato (she claims descent from Polish aristocracy), placed a large advertisement in the national English newspaper *The Guardian* on 19 July 1993 in which she warned the world that a 'huge cosmic event is due soon, namely the great cosmic explosion of a giant comet in our solar system'. According to press reports, Shoemaker-Levy 9 was first discovered by three American astronomers on 24 March 1993. In her announcement, however, Sofia Richmond claimed that she had published a 'cosmic forecast seven years ago on 4 July 1986 in all the north-west London newspapers that a huge cosmic event is due soon'.

Following her first notice, Richmond placed several more expensive advertisements in national newspapers in which she gave dramatic warnings to humanity. When the comet hit Jupiter, she stated, it would be a 'cosmic day of judg- ment for all mankind ... a warning ultimatum from almighty God'. 'Each person will see their life judged by God ... and each individual will see all the evil they have committed.' Various famous celebrities would experience conversions to Christianity, including the pop star 'the American Madonna'. Richmond also maintained that the comet was a broken fragment of Halley's Comet with a tail which could 'grow up to 100 million miles long', and that Jupiter 'could look like a second sun in the heavens'. In the small print on one of the announcements were the ominous words: 'People who persecuted Sister Marie or who ridi- culed God's message will suffer direct and instant retribu- tion from God on the day of the cosmic blast.'

Richmond's admonitions included the following advice: 'Adults and children should wear dark glasses for safety between 15–20 July . . . It would be advisable to stay in cold cellars or basements to avoid any heatwave . . . Keep curtains drawn and turn on air conditioning . . . Buy food for 5 days and keep pets indoors . . . Don't drive cars, lorries, buses or trains in case comet/Jupiter affects traffic.'

Following the physical collision between Jupiter and the comet, it became clear that the warnings and readings of Sofia Richmond were inaccurate. Further, her claim to have forecast the collision in advance of the American astronomers remains questionable. However, all this is of secondary interest to the new 'commandments'—allegedly given by God to mankind through Richmond—which, according to her pronouncements, should have been adhered to if disaster from the comet was to have been averted. In this 'warning ultimatum from God to all governments' are included the demands to: 'Reduce crime as in Saudi Arabia . . . Ban all indecency, obscenity, immodesty in public or in films, videos or television . . . Replace beers and wines with non-alcoholic drinks to reduce crime . . . Teach all schoolchildren moral laws and the ten commandments . . . Women must obey strict modesty laws in public to reduce sex crimes . . . All serious crimes to be punished by draconian deterrents.' One of the more bizarre commands was that people should 'become pure innocent angelic saints overnight'.

Sofia Richmond also predicted that: 'The warning explosion of the comet will herald a royal *coup d'état* and a royal revolution in England.' In her self-published book *Supernatural Visions of the Madonna 1981/1991* (1993) this prophecy is presented as the solution to the United Kingdom's social, political and religious problems.

So where does Sofia Richmond receive her information? The reclusive Catholic nun, who lives a contemplative solitary life in north London, claims to have regular contacts

with the divine Madonna. Her communications with the
Virgin Mary have purportedly been regular since a visit to
Lourdes in 1962 when she was told that she would take on
the mission of St Bernadette. Over the past ten years the
Madonna has appeared to Richmond six times. 'The Holy
Spirit gives enlightenment. It is an inspirational flash of
light. You have the absolute conviction.'[3]

It is not necessary here to enter into conjecture as to which
spiritual forces lie at the source of Sofia Richmond's
'inspirational' flashes. Certainly, through spiritual-scientific knowledge, one could adequately identify spiritual
beings that are likely to work within such situations today,
bringing impulses of this kind. In this case, however, it is
more valuable and revealing to study the 'warning ultimatum from God' which Richmond gives as a solution to
the problems of social life. This 'ultimatum' can be viewed
as a symptom of the present state of the spiritual stream that
Richmond represents; for her solutions—which rely, in her
own words, on 'draconian punishments'—seek ultimately
to force the human being to live an 'ordered' and 'good' life
through outward political and religious repression. Within
such political-religious ideas we can recognize a degenerate
impulse which arises from a thinking more in tune with the
intellectual-soul development of humanity. Such an
approach is, in modern times, directly opposed to the
development of the consciousness soul, which requires that
each person develops 'ethical individualism'—in the sense
of Rudolf Steiner's *Philosophy of Freedom*—in order for a
healthy social structure to be created out of freedom and
love.

As we approach the end of our troubled century, and
with it the onslaught of the adversary forces which Rudolf
Steiner spoke about many times, it is perhaps not surprising
that some people should respond to urgent social questions
with outmoded and backward-looking answers. It is
somewhat alarming, however, that such a resolution, which

so blatantly harks back to medieval social forms more akin
to fundamentalist Islam (where the religious and cultural
life rules the political, social and economic spheres), should
come in the name of Christianity.

2
BEAVIS AND BUTT-HEAD

The Ahrimanization of the Consciousness Soul

Before the first image of the programme flickers onto the television screen, the incessant manic laughter of the characters is heard: 'Huh huh huh—heh-heh m heh-heh—huh huh huh—heh-heh m heh-heh...' As the theme music begins their angular faces appear in profile, mouths dropping open to discharge rasps of nervous snickering. This is *Beavis and Butt-head*, one of the biggest successes of the cable music channel MTV (Music Television), which is screened around the world on American and European MTV, and also sold to other television channels such as Channel 4 in Britain.

MTV—an institution which is now as established a part of international American culture as Coca-Cola—is devoted to screening popular music. It first enjoyed success in the 1980s by utilizing the music-video, which the record companies had invented as a means of promoting popular music to a predominantly young audience. Videos—which allow music to be accompanied by visual moving images—are a crucial marketing tool for music companies to promote and sell their products. As pop music entered its fourth decade in the 1980s, it faced an increasingly apathetic youth audience—more thrilled by electronic televisual games than music—and the music-video became a crucial means of breaking through the new generation's seemingly listless consciousness.

Recorded music is already one step from the reality of live music. The music-video, with its mini-narratives and abstract images, increases that reality gap. *Beavis and Butt-*

head takes this whole twentieth-century experience one step further. The viewer of the programme sees the heroes—two crudely drawn cartoon characters, teenage boys named 'Beavis' and 'Butt-head'—watching music-videos. The viewer sees the videos as if he is watching with Beavis and Butt-head, and hears the characters' voices imposed over the music, giving a commentary to the sounds and visuals. From time to time Beavis and Butt-head appear on the screen themselves, sitting on a tattered armchair, watching television.

In the scenario of the show it is Beavis and Butt-head who control what is being seen on the screen, for they have the remote-control box which allows them to flick channels when they get bored. And they get bored often—or simply do not approve of what is being shown. Through this format, the viewer of the programme is given a constant subjective exposition of the music. However, the criticism of Beavis and Butt-head is somewhat crude, and their vocabulary strikingly limited. The videos are deemed to be either 'cool' (i.e. good) or they 'suck' (are bad). To add emphasis, Butt-head will occasionally exclaim: 'What the hell is this crap?'—or, alternatively, when a band is endorsed, he will state that such and such a band 'rules'.

As music critics Beavis and Butt-head are ruthlessly select in their tastes. For the most part they favour only the loudest and fastest guitar-based rock music (often referred to as 'thrash', 'death-metal', or 'hardcore') and the most bellicose rap (spoken rhymed lyrics over a heavy beat). Standard pop music is reviled, as is anything not overtly energetic and aggressive.

Spliced within all this music-video viewing are the remarkable adventures and antics of the two teenage cartoon characters. Two different narratives are shown every week, each about 15 minutes long. One week they are asked to prune the branches of a neighbouring old man's tree in return for a small payment. Taking a chainsaw they saw the trunk of the enormous tree which then falls on the man's house. Their response to the calamity, amidst fits of giggles, is: 'I'm afraid we're going to have to charge you extra, sir, for demolishing your house.' In another episode they decide to 'couch-fish' and, sitting back on their armchair, cast a fishing-line out of the window. After pulling in a live racoon, followed by a school acquaintance (with the fishing-hook caught through his thumb), they drag in an old woman who has been tempted by the 'bait' of a prune box. In another adventure entitled 'Car Wash' they are given the task of washing a 1959 Corvette, the prize possession of a neighbour. Finding the keys they drive the car away and cause a serious road accident. Sitting in the wrecked Corvette, with flames erupting around them, their only response is: 'Whoa—that was cool.'

In an officially sanctioned book, *Beavis and Butt-head, This Book Sucks*,[1] we are given a view of the characters' formative years. Beavis is pictured as a five-year-old boy pouring lighter-fluid on his birthday cake to make his 'wish come true'. At age nine he is depicted holding a baseball bat with a squashed frog stuck to the bottom. Elsewhere cruelty to insects is justified by an 'Insect Court' chart which shows a picture of the insect (e.g. 'Daddy Longlegs from backyard') and the 'crime' ('loitering'), the 'verdict' ('guilty'), and the 'punishment' ('de-legged; death by magnifying glass'). Violence is never far from view in the book: one image shows the two smashing a private mailbox with baseball bats. The volume, packaged in gaudy colours to attract a youth readership, also includes some of Beavis's and Butt-head's more intellectual thoughts: for example their attempts to compose verse in the traditional Japanese Haiku style. One sample runs: 'It's cool not to suck / 'Cause I don't like stuff that sucks / I like stuff that's cool.' An essay on the subject 'Freedom and what have I done to deserve it' is also featured, and includes the following: 'Kicking Beavis's ass, blowing up stuff, watching TV, hanging out at the convenience store, or the park. That is what freedom means to me . . .'

Of course, Beavis and Butt-head are both cartoon characters that do not, as such, exist in 'real life'. MTV are very keen to emphasize this fact in response to mounting criticism of the programme. Thus each episode begins with a disclaimer, stating that Beavis and Butt-head are not 'role models'. This is reiterated in the book, which elaborates: '. . . they're not even human. They're cartoons. Some of the things they do would cause a real person to get hurt, expelled, arrested, possibly deported. To put it another way: Don't try this at home.' MTV have good reason to be concerned. The American edition of *Time* magazine (25 October 1993) reported that an Ohio mother had charged that certain episodes of the programme—which portrayed the two characters gleefully planning pranks with fire—incited her five-year-old son to set their home ablaze, killing his two-year-old sister. As a result of this action MTV moved the show from 7 p.m. to 10.30 p.m.

In their analysis, *Time* magazine claimed that: 'The two cartoon nerds do not encourage stupidity and cruelty to animals: they satirize it.' From one point of view this argument could be justified, although it would be difficult to sustain. However, even if one does view the programme as a satirical critique of materialistic culture, it is nevertheless a fact that children—a significant portion of the programme's audience—generally do not understand satire. Moreover, due to their imitative qualities, children *are* likely to perceive the characters as 'role-models', and attempt to emulate their actions.

While literature of this century has provided us with many examples of rebellious youthful characters, celebrated and loved for their naughtiness—for example 'William' in the books by Richmal Crompton—nothing quite prepares us for the maliciousness and the complete lack of conscience displayed by the two teenage boys in *Beavis and*

Butt-head. We are presented here with a modern cultural phenomenon which, in its explicit and unashamed veneration of depravity, challenges us to come to a conscious understanding of it. To do this we must attempt to cognize the living forces behind the phenomenon, the process of which immediately raises questions. In this case we might ask: what is being depicted in *Beavis and Butt-head* in an occult sense, and what enables such a programme to be produced and promoted in our time as part of mainstream culture?

In addressing the first part of the question, we may be tempted to view the characters simply as idiotic, demented thugs or fools. Such an analysis would provide us with a seemingly satisfactory and conclusive answer, but it would not be accurate. Certainly, Beavis and Butt-head are not portrayed as being especially intelligent in an intellectual sense. However, they do manifest faculties that suggest a form of consciousness which, in terms of humanity's evolution, is modern in nature. In other words, they demonstrate an individual, or 'self', consciousness. We could also refer to this form of modern self-awareness as 'ego-consciousness'. In its most developed form such a consciousness enables the individual to act freely out of his or her own inner impulses, a situation which arises from an integration of the higher and lower selves of the human being. Relating Beavis and Butt-head to such a state of consciousness may initially seem perverse, but on closer inspection it can be seen to have validity.

Far from being fools, it is apparent that Beavis and Butt-head are intended by their creators to be clever, aware and awake. In their critique of the music-videos, for example, they exhibit a sharp black humour and alert wit, suggesting an ability for close observation. Their immoral inclinations are usually calculated and often have a sardonic, scheming aspect to them. In other words, ulterior motives are never far from view. (For example, in one episode Butt-head encourages Beavis to fake being hit by a car and then, pretending that his liver has been damaged in the accident, to ask the driver for an instant payment in return for a promise not to sue for damages.) Their destructive urges, while sometimes pure hooliganism, often suggest a creative faculty—an imagination which enables them continuously to discover new means to counteract their boredom. (See, for example, the episode 'Closing Time' in which they artistically 'decorate' the fast-food restaurant where they work by throwing food and drink at the over-head fan.)

And yet, despite demonstrating a close understanding of their deeds, Beavis and Butt-head know no remorse or conscience. On the contrary, all their actions are accom-panied with the repetitious machine-gun cackle of their laughter: 'Huh huh huh—Heh-heh m heh-heh.' These characteristics suggest what could be expressed as a form of evil related to ego-consciousness. Instructive in this respect is a published lecture by Manfred Schmidt-Brabant entitled 'An Anatomy of Violence' in which he designates four kinds of violence relating to the physical body, etheric body, astral body and the ego. Describing Rudolf Steiner's picture of the evolution of consciousness, Schmidt-Brabant emphasizes the necessity of individual and autonomous self-development in our present time. But this stage in humanity's progress creates serious difficulties and chal-lenges:

> Intensely strong spiritual forces are stirring because the time has come for the emancipation of the individuality. It follows that if these powers of individualization cannot come to expression in social life they will begin to degenerate and start to be destructive. As a result, a new kind of violence will generally come about. It is not astral and emotional, nor is it etheric and based on tempera-ment; it arises where ego development processes should

be taking place. The potential that can take humanity forward does exist but very often it cannot find positive expression, and so it degenerates and becomes destructive.[2]

In *Beavis and Butt-head* we can recognize such a substitution of 'ego development processes' with degenerate forces, allowing evil to be perpetrated with a new 'ego consciousness'—a state within which the human being is able freely to determine his actions. However, it is possible to take a further step by linking the behaviour of Beavis and Butt-head with a degeneration of the consciousness soul, i.e. that part of the human being which is able to develop, through clear objectivity and knowledge, a devotion to truth.

In a lecture given on 8 December 1918[3] Rudolf Steiner indicated that the English-speaking peoples are endowed with certain forces which impel them towards the consciousness soul. 'It is the case that this inclination towards the consciousness soul appears in them instinctively in an entirely different way than it does with other people.' However, this 'instinctive' emergence of the consciousness soul requires nurturing and development on the path of modern initiation, if it is not to languish and be corrupted. In his book *Knowledge of the Higher Worlds* Rudolf Steiner describes certain inner 'conditions' that are required as a preparation for inner development of this kind. But in Beavis and Butt-head we see, *par excellence*, the antithesis of such inner qualities. Instead of being reverent, respectful, devoted to truth, tolerant and objective, they are irreverent, sarcastic, cynical and intolerant. One could go further, but the point is clear: their crazed existence illustrates the opposite of the 'rich inner life' required from the modern spiritual student.

Of course it is not being suggested that a modern cartoon programme should depict characters on a path of inner development. Such an expectation would be naive. However, in *Beavis and Butt-head* much of what we see is in a certain sense diametrically opposed to human evolution. In its prophetic pictures we can perceive a tangible danger which threatens humanity if it does not begin to work consciously with its ego-forces, in particular with the forces of the consciousness soul. For, as Sergei O. Prokofieff elucidates in his work *The Spiritual Origins of Eastern Europe and the Future Mysteries of the Holy Grail*, if the consciousness soul—even when it is present in an 'instinctive' form—is not spiritualized, humanity '... will begin to develop in a downward direction towards an ever greater ahrimanization, in accordance with its affinity with man's physical body. In the latter eventuality, instead of an evolution towards the Spirit Self there would take place an ever greater fusing of the soul—as it became ahrimanized—with the physical body.'[4]

As has been suggested, this 'ahrimanized consciousness soul'—which is a particular danger to the English-speaking and other western peoples because of their intense immersion in an overtly consumption-orientated materialism—is already evident in an artistic form in *Beavis and Butt-head*. So why, to address the second part of our initial question, is such a pictorial representation of this ugly state of being so openly promoted and disseminated in our time? And why is such material so explicitly marketed to children who, as was stated earlier, are especially open to influence and suggestion?

From his spiritual research, Rudolf Steiner claimed that certain occult brotherhoods and lodges of the West systematically sponsor materialism in an attempt to hold humanity back from its evolutionary tasks. In Prokofieff's words:

> In order to perpetuate their authority in earthly evolution, an authority which they are able to exercise only in

the epoch of the consciousness soul (the fifth) the western lodges try by every available means not only to spread materialism in all its many forms throughout the whole of humanity but, at a higher level, to transform it into a kind of 'super-materialism', into a form of Americanism. By means of this they hope so to influence the development of the consciousness soul in the fifth post-Atlantean epoch that it will in future be simply unable to receive the Spirit Self.[5]

Such an eventuality would mean '...the arising of, on the one hand, a humanity which, to be sure, consists of separate individualities, but is on account of its being permeated by super-materialism devoid of any ethical roots...'[6] Whether or not we accept the possibility of the existence of occult groups with specific agendas as described above, we can certainly see that individuals lacking any kind of morality or ethics are already present, in a fictional form, in *Beavis and Butt-head*.

When confronted with the above fact, and the realization that this ahrimanized, animalistic picture of man is promoted with such effrontery, we may be led to ask sincerely whether it is really possible—given the weight of the adversary forces—for humanity to advance and mature further in our time out of its own inner forces. This is the 'true Parsifal question' of today, the central question of our time, which Prokofieff formulates as follows:

> ...Does the ever-intensifying individualization of man in modern times, arising out of the consciousness soul, bring to earthly evolution only evil, destruction, moral decadence and interminable outpourings of wild, antisocial instincts, or is this quality of human individuality, in its ever-greater freedom from all outward norms, laws, precepts, traditions and prescriptions, capable of giving birth out of itself to higher moral ideals and new socially active impulses which will then at the same time be the

moral ideals and social impulses of the Christ amongst mankind?[7]

Of course, the programme *Beavis and Butt-head* is not in itself responsible for the present dangers facing humanity. However, it does perform the function of providing us with a clear picture of the abyss—of the hazards that arise as a consequence of greater individualization. In doing this it delineates the challenge posed to every conscious, spiritually striving human being. This challenge can be taken up through a living wisdom of the world and humanity—an Anthroposophy based on inner knowledge and conviction—enabling every person to take an active part in the battle for the future. From our own experience we may then be able address this 'Parsifal question' and, from an esoteric certitude, confirm that it can indeed be answered in the affirmative.

3
FILMS, VIOLENCE, AND 'REALITY' IN ART

In June 1995 the film *Reservoir Dogs*—the directorial debut of the 31-year-old American Quentin Tarantino—was finally given a video release in England. Although first shown in cinemas in 1992, the distributors of *Reservoir Dogs* had been refused permission until then to release the film on video by the British Board of Film Classification because of its violent content.

Made on a low budget, with most of the action taking place in an empty warehouse, *Reservoir Dogs* depicts the struggles and recriminations between a gang of criminals in the aftermath of a failed armed robbery. The most notorious scene shows the beating and torture of a captured policeman by one of the criminal gang. In the film's climactic moment the psychopathic ex-convict, knife in hand, slices off the ear of his bound and gagged prisoner. Tarantino's clever touch is to accompany the macabre scene not by eerie or thrilling music, but by the mellow strains of a 1970s pop song (*Stuck in the Middle With You*, by Steelers Wheel) to which his maniacal character dances and jiggles as he anticipates carrying out the merciless act.

This bizarre juxtaposition of mellifluous music and extreme violence has led, at the peak of the film's torture scene, to people walking out of cinemas in revulsion. Tarantino's response to the evident disgust of some of his audience is unmoved: 'It never bothered me when people walked out. It just meant that scene worked ... I'm not interested in making a cartoon. I'm interested in making the violence real.'[1] Indeed, Stuart Gordon—the director of *Re-Animator* (a classic 'horror' movie)—reportedly told Tarantino after witnessing *Reservoir Dogs*: 'Quentin, I walked out of your movie, but I want you to take it as a compliment. See, we all deal in fantasy. There's no such thing as were-wolfs or vampires. You're dealing with real-life violence, and I can't deal with it.'[2]

In 1994 Tarantino's follow-up film *Pulp Fiction* was shown at the Cannes Film Festival where it won the Palme d'Or. While *Pulp Fiction* is a more commercial and accessible film than its predecessor, Tarantino had no intention of compromising on the violent content: the film features shootings, stabbings, sadomasochism and homosexual rape. (It also portrays heroin injection and a drug overdose of its main female character.) Defending his film from accusations of gratuitous violence, Tarantino declared: 'Gratuitous violence [in films] is when they do it bad ... and it's lame. I don't know what gratuitous violence is.'[3]

On this point rival director Oliver Stone would agree with him. His film *Natural Born Killers*, which tells of the murderous jaunt of a young couple across America who kill 52 people before being arrested, was refused a certificate by the British Board of Film Classification for three months while it investigated allegations that the film had inspired ten murders. Stone, a veteran film-maker whose previous work includes *Platoon* and *JFK*, states: 'I don't believe in avoiding violence because it's part of life.' Echoing Tarantino, he adds: 'If you're going to show an act of violence it should really be authentic and real and scary. You aim a gun, blood spurts everywhere.'[4]

In terms of explicit violence in modern cinema, it should clearly be stated that none of the above films rival the excesses of 'splatter' horror movies such as *Friday the 13th*, *Nightmare on Elm Street*, or numerous others in that vein, which include many scenes of bloody violence. However, while for the most part the horror genre is treated with disdain by critics, and viewed as the 'fast food' of the film industry—cheap and nasty trash for the masses—Tarantino's films are respected as serious works of art. The

Guardian film critic, for example, described *Pulp Fiction* as 'a piece of genuine brilliance … with an unerring mastery over every aspect of the film-maker's craft'.[5]

Certainly Tarantino has a unique talent for directing and script-writing. In *Pulp Fiction* he masterfully weaves together the threads of three narratives, moving forwards and backwards in time, while certain scenes are repeated to allow the audience to view events from different points of view. And yet the film includes macabre scenes of ruthless killing. In one instance two gangsters, Jules and Vincent, are sent to execute members of a rival drug ring. After terrifying his unarmed victims with pointed questions, Jules— with an air of self-righteous indignation—booms out biblical Old Testament verses ('And I will execute great vengeance upon them with furious rebukes; and they shall know that I am the Lord, when I shall lay my vengeance upon them')[6] before the two killers pump dozens of bullets into the bodies of their victims. What gives the scene such an uncanny edge is that minutes before carrying out the execution the two men had been discussing what a McDonald's Big Mac is called in France, and whether or not a foot-massage is to be considered erotic. Apart from the Old Testament mock-dramatics, the murders are carried out with seeming indifference—as one might set about any slightly tiresome job.

Is such a depiction of grim murder valid? One could argue that much highly respected drama includes violence; for example, Shakespeare's historical dramas and tragedies are littered with premeditated brutal murders. Many key characters exhibit an evil intent and conspire to bring about the death of others (see, for example, Iago in *Othello*). Could it not reasonably be said that the mass-murderer Macbeth is something of a 'natural born killer' in the tradition of Oliver Stone's serial killers? This argument is difficult to sustain, however, if one takes more than a cursory glance at the differences between the drama of Shakespeare and the drama of Tarantino. For while some of Shakespeare's plays include or allude to explicit acts of violence, they are always placed within the context of a detailed study of the human condition. Through complex and elaborate character portrayals, which are often presented on a soul and spirit level, Shakespeare allows us to comprehend the intricacies of human life and destiny. Indeed, in the best of Shakespeare we are given wonderful pictorial archetypes of our humanity. For example, in the case of Hamlet we see— according to Rudolf Steiner's research—the individuality of the Trojan commander Hector who, as a consequence of the Mystery of Golgotha, is a soul struggling with the necessity of experiencing individual ego-consciousness in his present incarnation.[7] By presenting us with significant aspects of our own evolution, Shakespeare enables us, through this wider perspective, to assimilate the tragic and violent aspects of his drama.

In contrast, Tarantino does not allow us to penetrate the psyche of his characters. They are given little background, motive, context or spiritual depth. As critic James Wood observes: 'He [Tarantino] represents the final triumph of post-modernism, which is to empty the artwork of all content, thus voiding its capacity to do anything except helplessly *represent* our agonies ... Only in this age could a writer as talented as Tarantino produce artworks so entirely vacuous, so stripped of any politics, metaphysics, or moral interest.'[8]

The stock defence by many serious film-makers to this point, and to the whole question of explicit violence in films, is that somehow their task is simply to 'reflect reality'. Following this argument the modern film-maker is thereby justified in portraying the most sickening violence. Thus Tarantino says of *Reservoir Dogs*: 'I think one of the strengths of the film is that it is realistic.'[9] Or Oliver Stone, explaining the violence in *Natural Born Killers*, states that: 'The world is violent, and we're swamped in it in this century. So I mirror that...'[10] In another interview Stone, when challenged on the point of whether his film merely adds to a culture of violence, responds: 'So what if it's part of the problem? You don't have to have a solution in a work of art.'[11]

In contemplating the above we may be led to pose a number of related questions. Firstly, is the role of art simply to 'reflect reality'? Secondly, what is the nature of this perceived 'reality'? And thirdly, to what extent does this 'reality' contribute to and create the 'reality' of materialism in which our culture is presently immersed?

Reflecting 'reality'

In considering the first question, the conversation between Sophia and Estella in the Prelude to Rudolf Steiner's first Mystery Drama, *The Portal of Initiation,* is instructive. Estella is attempting to convince her friend to accompany her to a performance of a play which, she feels, is 'genuine art' that 'lays hold of the very essence of our lives'.[12] Sophia, the member of a spiritual society that is also giving its own dramatic performance the same evening, is reserved about her friend's enthusiasm, stating that 'there may be people who call your "living reality" actually poverty-stricken... You have no conception of the living, creative spirit that forms human beings with the same elemental power as the germinating forces in Nature form a seed.'[13] Furthermore, Sophia is convinced that human beings can only realize their ideals if they connect 'what they call reality and life with those deeper [spiritual] experiences which you've often termed fantastic, wild imaginings.'[14] For Sophia (and, we may conclude, for Rudolf Steiner) much of modern drama 'is only fruitless criticism of life. For no hunger is stilled, no tears are dried, no source of moral degradation is uncovered, when merely the outer appearance of hunger or tear-stained faces or degraded characters are shown on stage. How this is usually done is unspeakably distant from the real depths of life and the true relationships between living beings.'[15]

In an earlier 'sketch' for the Prelude, in which Estella and Sophia are replaced with a married couple, the wife says of modern drama to her husband: '...it seems to reflect everyday life that is unfortunately so empty! Why should I be intrigued by uninteresting characters on the stage who are manipulated like sleepwalkers? I am bored even by the new drama which pretends to be bursting with vitality. It is either without content—rightly so, because it mirrors truthfully our present time—or else it is a strong criticism of life, and, as such, is pretty futile.'[16] The husband is defensive, stating that the triumph of modern art is that it 'no longer tries to rise into idealistic dream-spheres but actually reflects the struggles of our daily life.'[17]

Rudolf Steiner could as well have written the above as a commentary to Tarantino's films. In fact the critic James Wood, quoted earlier, comes to the same conclusions as Steiner's spiritually-minded characters. *Pulp Fiction*, he says, represents the 'final triumph of post-modernism, which is to empty the artwork of all content.'[18] We could add that Tarantino's characters 'are manipulated like sleepwalkers', and that the drama offers (in the words of Sophia) 'no conception of the living, creative spirit that forms human beings'.

A distorted 'reality' and its effects

So what, we may then ask, is the nature of the 'reality' that is reflected in films such as *Pulp Fiction* and *Reservoir Dogs*? As early as 1917 Rudolf Steiner observed that 'there is no better school for materialism than the cinema'.[19] One could interpret these words in a number of ways, but in the case of Quentin Tarantino they can be taken and applied quite literally. For Tarantino—who has had no formal training in drama or film-making—represents an unprecedented generation of film-makers that has been 'schooled' by the medium which it seeks to create, a so-called 'out-of-the-video-stores-and-onto-the-screens' movement. As Tarantino's friend Roger Avary, director of *Killing Zoe*, puts it: 'There's a fresh generation of film-makers, and they're coming out of the video stores. All of us have the advantage of a data base of thousands of movies.'[20]

Already as a youth Tarantino spent hours at the cinema. 'Basically, I spent my life at the movies',[21] he says candidly. Later he became an usher in a pornographic film theatre, and then finally got a job working in a Los Angeles video shop. 'I basically lived there for years. We'd get off work, close up store, then sit around and watch movies all night.'[22] On Fridays he and his friends would 'plot things out so we could see all four new movies we were interested in.'[23] This obsession with film continues for Tarantino today. When asked what his typical day consists of, he replies: 'I go to movies, sometimes more than once a day, and I watch TV with friends. Occasionally, I go to coffee shops. That and work. That's what I do.'[24]

What can be the result of this self-perpetuating 'school' of modern cinema other than that it begins to create its own 'reality'? James Wood notes that in *Pulp Fiction* many of the lines and situations are borrowed wholesale from other films. In fact, he concludes, 'the entire film is in quotation marks'.[25] (Indeed, the stage directions for the opening scene run: 'Their dialogue is to be said in a rapid-pace *His Girl Friday* fashion.')[26] If, therefore, in this derivative and self-referential vortex, art begins to create its own illusory reality, to what extent, we may reasonably ask, does it in turn begin to create the 'reality' of the culture within which we live? In connection to our theme we may rephrase this to read: to what extent does violence in films create violence in real life? This complex question has sparked a debate which has raged, and will continue to rage, for many years—particularly in America—and cannot be resolved here.[27] Although various studies have been made, direct 'proof' of a link between screen violence and violence in society is difficult to obtain. Nevertheless, we can draw our own conclusions as to what effect the depiction of an act of violence has when it is stripped of any real background or motive, and when it is divorced from its consequences of suffering, grief and pain. In a special report on violence in films and music, *Time* magazine repeated the words of a 15-year-old boy, picked at random in a fast-food restaurant: 'I liked the part in *Pulp Fiction* where the guy points a gun and says a prayer from the Bible and then kills everybody. You hear the gun go *brrr*. It's cool.'[28] Such reactions are not surprising, as in both *Pulp Fiction* and *Natural Born Killers* gun violence is carried out with a leisurely nonchalance that helps to glamorize such acts, making them potentially attractive. The gun as a weapon—already something of a modern icon—is glorified as a mighty force of omnipotent power and authority.

The effects of the cinema

When speaking of the cinema, Rudolf Steiner stated that 'what one sees there is not reality as we see it. Only an age which has so little idea of reality as this age of ours, which worships reality as an idol in a material sense, could believe that the cinema represents reality.'[29] He goes on to ask his audience which they believe is closer to reality: a picture painted by an artist of a person walking along a street, or a filmed sequence of the same scene. 'If you put the question to yourself honourably, you will admit that what the artist produces in a state of rest is much more like what you see. Hence, while people are sitting at the cinema, what they see there does not make its way into the ordinary faculty of perception; it enters a deeper, more material stratum than we usually employ for our perception.'[30]

And here we are led to a second phenomenon which arises from our study as another symptom of the state of modern cinema. For while Tarantino is content simply to reflect 'reality' as he sees it, Oliver Stone's pretentious ideas in *Natural Born Killers* lead him to create an insidious sub-liminal method which subdues our ability to counteract what we see on the screen, and hence works more strongly on this 'deep material stratum' that Steiner refers to. In a bid to mirror what he calls the 'collective unconscious for the century'[31] Stone uses the device of creating a swirling kaleidoscope of images—switching from black-and-white to colour, from Super 8 and standard film to animation—with back projections, fast editing, and a loud rock-music soundtrack. This form, according to Stone, '...serves two purposes. It reflects the junkyard culture of the time, it has a TV sensibility where everything is changing, channel-surfing, coming at you. But stylistically, we also wanted to enter into the heads of the two killers, make it subjective, hallucinatory. They've watched a lot of TV. They're desensitized to it.'[32] Elsewhere he says: 'We wanted to put the audience right in the driver's seat—make them the killers. Virtual reality goggles, so to speak, where you would participate, you would enjoy the ride...'[33] While Stone might believe he is somehow exposing 'junkyard culture' with this technique, in actuality he is, ironically, only adding to it by lulling his audience's consciousness to the pictures being projected on the screen.

Psychological 'reality'

When asked in an interview if *Natural Born Killers* is an amoral film, Stone retorts: 'No, the film is moral in that it posits the notion that killing is inevitable in the environment that has grown up... The reasons for violence are social: poverty, neglect, lack of family, huge arms sales abroad and at home...'[34] Among the jumble of images in his film, Stone interjects his own attempts to *explain* the cultural crisis of our time. Yet his tool for comprehending the mayhem of mass-murder is modern materialistic pop-psychology. For example, to elucidate the viciousness of Mallory—his murderous female heroine—he shows scenes from her abused childhood. But the messages are super-ficial, confused and contradictory. Adding to the twentieth-century stream of mechanized consciousness, these images are flippantly presented in the style of an American 'situation comedy', complete with pre-recorded laughter. And before the viewer is able fully to comprehend this psychological interpretation, the film abruptly turns into a satire of the media and its presentation of violence. In contrast to the cynical and manipulative media, the killers Mickey and Mallory—now imprisoned—are viewed as innocents. Mickey is allowed to present his thoughts as to why he is a mass-murderer. In relation to the decadent world around him an act of murder, he says, is 'pure'. Mickey has realized his 'true calling in life': 'I'm a natural born killer,' he drawls contentedly.

As we see from the above, Oliver Stone presents us with images of extreme violence, but purports to give some analysis and explanation. In doing so, however, he is unable to uncover, in Sophia's words, 'the living, creative spirit that forms human beings', and the result—a confused blur of 'meaningful' pictures, against which the viewer has to battle to retain his individual consciousness—is arguably more dangerous that the honest 'living reality' of Tarantino.

Counterbalancing the effects of the cinema

When talking of the cinema, Steiner was keen, as always, to balance his negative observations, emphasizing that the world is confronted with impulses that lead to materialism as part of the 'deep needs of the age'. While the cinema has a materializing effect—through the human being's etheric body—on his consciousness and his deepest sub-consciousness, humanity could at the same time 'develop an ascent above it, an ascent into spiritual reality. Then the cinema will do him no harm, and he [the human being] can see it as often as he likes. But unless the counterbalance is there, people will be led by such things as these not to have their proper relation to the earth, but to become more and more closely related to it, until at last they are entirely shut off from the spiritual world.'[35]

Clearly, Rudolf Steiner is talking here of counter-balancing phenomena like the cinema with spiritual work: meditation, the study of spiritual science, and the devel-opment of a living relationship to the reality of the spirit in our everyday lives. However, in a conversation reported by Pieter de Hahn and related by Emanuel Zeylmans, Steiner is also purported to have said that it would be good if anthroposophists were to make films, and that it would be a particularly suitable medium to show the laws of karma as they work in successive incarnations.[36]

In recent times a number of films have been made that successfully portray something of the intricate complexities of the destinies of individuals and their relationships (see, for example, Atom Egoyan's *Exotica*, Kieslowski's *Three Colours Red*, or Robert Altman's *Short Cuts*). While some of these films offer useful insights into the human condition, they all fall short of the above challenge posed by Rudolf Steiner: that precise knowledge of reincarnation and karma be brought to the medium of film.

The anthroposophical movement may have access to the 'living creative spirit that forms human beings' in the shape of Rudolf Steiner's four Mystery Dramas, Goethe's *Faust*, and so on, but this truly immense Manichaean task—of bringing concrete knowledge of reincarnation and karma to the sphere of the cinema—stands before it as a challenge. And it becomes ever more urgent as elements of spiritual reality begin to creep, in an inevitably distorted form, into Hollywood's commercial film-machine (see, for example, Kenneth Branagh's fictional account of reincarnation, *Dead Again*).

Only through fulfilling this task, one suspects, will humanity be able fully to redeem the more dangerous aspects of the cinema we have been considering above—the poverty-stricken 'reality' of Tarantino, and the inadequate and incomplete psychology of Oliver Stone. And it is those who have access to the treasure of Anthroposophy who have the tools to transform and redeem these aspects of technology and materialism, so that they may become reassimilated into the true destiny of human evolution.

4
GANGSTA RAP, REALITY AND 'SUPERMATERIALISM'

In the beginning of June 1995 the Republican and majority leader of the US Senate, Bob Dole, made a direct attack on the corporate giant Time Warner for its part in the promotion of degenerate culture. 'We have reached the point where our popular culture threatens to undermine our character as a nation,' he said. 'Those who cultivate moral confusion for profit should understand this: we will name their names and shame them as they deserve to be shamed.' Dole mentioned the films *Natural Born Killers* and *True Romance,* and cited a sub-genre of popular music known as 'gangsta [*sic*] rap'. True to his word, he went on to name Warner Brothers' subsidiary record label Interscope (of which Time Warner has a 50 per cent share), which has on its roster some of rap's most popular artists such as Snoop Doggy Dogg, Dr Dre, and Tupac. 'You have sold your souls, but must you debase our nation and threaten our children for the sake of corporate profits?'[1] Bob Dole asked Time Warner executives rhetorically.*

Two weeks earlier William Bennett, the former Secretary of Education, and C. DeLores Tucker, head of the National Political Congress of Black Women, had taken their campaign against violent and explicit lyrics—also focusing on gangsta rap—to the annual Time Warner shareholders' meeting. 'At one point in the meeting,' *Time* magazine reported, 'Tucker rose from the audience and delivered a

---

* Subsequent to the writing of this article, on 27 September 1995, Time Warner announced that it was going to sell its 50% stake in Interscope.

17-minute attack on violent and misogynistic lyrics in songs recorded by Time Warner performers. At the end of her speech, about a third of the packed audience burst into applause.'[2] Around the same time the Speaker of the US House of Representatives, Newt Gingrich, informed *Time* editors that major radio advertisers should band together to boycott stations that played 'explicitly vicious' rap.[3]

Political commentators seemed to agree that Dole's speech was cynically designed to attract support from the Christian right—particularly Ralph Reed's Christian Coalition. Nevertheless his comments, and also those of Gingrich, Tucker and Bennett, are significant; for while outrage against youth culture by major public figures is not a new phenomenon, such close attention to one particular type of music is rare.

So what is gangsta rap and why is it causing such a commotion? While such a question could be studied on many levels, only an attempt to perceive precisely how occult forces work behind the manifestation and develop-ment of such phenomena can allow us to approach a full understanding. To achieve such insight it is necessary to study the history and development of rap, and in particular the process through which gangsta rap came to emerge as such a dominating force in modern music.

Since the explosion of rock 'n' roll in the 1950s, popular music has been one of the most influential mediums within youth culture. However, the lyrical content of the vast majority of recordings has concentrated on the same sub-jects: love and sexuality. Some artists have attempted to use music to communicate other ideas—often of a social or political nature—and this became noticeably evident, for example, in the 1960s with the rise of the 'hippie' move-ment. With the advent of 'punk rock' in 1976 this trend towards social commentary accelerated. Although some punk groups had unfocused and unclear intentions—basing their appeal on raw energy, anger and rebellion—

others like the Clash and the Jam had political agendas. When the Sex Pistols reached number one in the pop charts during the week of the Royal Jubilee celebrations in 1977 with their irreverent anti-monarchist single 'God Save the Queen', pop music's potential as an anti-establishment force became apparent.

And yet, despite the embarrassment that the hippies, punks and other youth movements have caused the establishment over the years, pop music has been largely ineffective as an agent for genuine social change. This could partly be attributed to the fact that the classic three-minute pop song is not ideal for the communication and development of serious or complex ideas. However, in the mid-1970s this situation was to change with the birth of a new genre within popular music that took the name 'rap' or 'hip hop'. This sound, which emerged from the black New York ghetto of the Bronx, featured a 'rapper' who would speak lyrics, rhythmically and in rhyme, over a backbeat produced by a DJ (disc jockey) manipulating two copies of the same record on double turntables. Where previously the pop vocalist's capacity for expression was limited by the form of the song and the need to sing, this new type of vocal delivery freed the 'rapper' to express him or herself at length over the rhythm.

With the release of the record *Rapper's Delight* by the Sugar Hill Gang in 1979, which went on to sell over two million copies, rap was instantly transformed from an underground black urban culture to an international commercial commodity. Lyrically, the content of rap records remained very much within the black tradition of street slang and word-battles known as 'the dozens' and 'signifying'.[4] The rapper would speak of his own prowess and bravado, his skills and wealth, and 'dis' (show disrespect to) his opponents and competitors. But this situation began to change in 1982 when a new type of rap emerged with the release of *The Message* by Grandmaster Flash and the

Furious Five (Sugar Hill Records). With its strikingly vivid first person account of the urban ghetto, *The Message* was the first rap record to attempt a social commentary: '...I can't take the smell, can't take the noise / Got no money to move out, I guess I got no choice / Rats in the front room, roaches in the back / Junkies in the alley with a baseball bat...'

Although a number of hit rap records followed over the next few years, the artform remained something of a novelty to the mainstream market. However, when the rap group Run-DMC teamed up with the American rock band Aerosmith to cover their song 'Walk this Way', rap gained exposure through MTV (Music Television) and broke through to the white mass market. Meanwhile, the beats and music of rap—which had initially relied on the basic live 'sampling' of old records by a DJ—had become more sophisticated and complex with the aid of studio trickery and recording techniques. Record companies were now forced to take note of a phenomenon which many had written off as a gimmick.

While the traditional brand of self-aggrandizing rap continued, a new school of rappers—inspired by the social concerns of *The Message*—gradually emerged. This new school, which included groups like Public Enemy, BDP and Gang Starr, was concerned with questions of 'consciousness', identity and positivity within the black community.[5] The messages and discussion on these new rap records were directed by black artists to their own people but, as fascination and interest in rap grew among white music buyers, a much wider public was listening. Vocalist Chuck D of the group Public Enemy was well aware of this, proclaiming on one of his recordings that his intention was to 'reach the Bourgeois, and rock the boulevard [the streets]'.[6]

Rap now stood at a crossroads in its development. While the market had expanded with the success of the 'conscious' rappers, the dynamic nature of the artform continued to encourage new styles. Simultaneously, two new types of rap developed: the whimsical, off-beat and intelligent humour of groups such as De La Soul and A Tribe Called Quest, and the violent aggression and rage of what came to be called gangsta rap. Aside from the ever present black rap fans, the former style gained much favour from the 'college' student audience, while the latter—with its macho descriptions of 'black on black' (gang) violence, drinking, drug-dealing, misogynistic sexuality, and the clamouring for material wealth—began to entice the now mainstream rap market of white, middle-class teenagers.

Although the origins of gangsta rap can be traced back to pioneers of the sound such as Schoolly D, the first record to epitomize its extreme nature was *Straight Outta Compton* (Ruthless Records, 1988) by an unknown group called NWA (Niggers with Attitude). *Straight Outta Compton*, which has since sold over two million copies, is a dirty and raw celebration of criminal street life. Littered with expletives, it deliberately mocks the 'conscious' and constructive rap which was popular at the time of its release. On 'Gangsta Gangsta', for example, Ice Cube asks: 'Do I look like a mother****in' role model? / To a kid looking up to me, life ain't nothin' but bitches and money'; while on the title track he boasts: '... I got a sawn-off [shotgun] / squeeze the trigger and bodies are hauled off ... Here's a murder rap to keep you dancin' / With a crime record like Charles Manson / AK47 is the tool—don't make me act the mother****in' fool ...'

Straight Outta Compton provided the inspiration for a forgotten generation of socially deprived black youth, and as a consequence a whole host of gangsta rappers was born, including such names as the Geto Boys, Spice 1 and Compton's Most Wanted. Encouraged by record companies, who saw that this new product could be effectively marketed, the new breed seemingly battled each other to make the most outrageous, violent and shocking records.

When the group Cypress Hill released their eponymous debut album (Ruff House Records, 1991) featuring such tracks as 'How I Could Just Kill a Man', 'Hand on the Pump' and 'Hole in the Head', *The Source* magazine praised them for their 'sincerity and self-expression', and 'unique approach'.[7] Many blacks, however, were not so impressed. The frequent use in gangsta rap of the racist term 'nigger'— appropriated from white supremists as black street slang— and numerous references to women as 'bitches' and 'hos' (whores) were particular irritants.

Gangsta rap has since become a huge source of revenue for the music industry. The debut album by Dr Dre entitled *The Chronic* (Death Row Records, 1993), which includes songs such as 'A Nigga Witta Gun' and 'Rat-Tat-Tat-Tat', has to date sold over four million copies. His protégé Snoop Doggy Dogg had pre-release orders of over a million copies for his album *Doggy Style* (Death Row Records, 1993), which swiftly went on to emulate sales of *The Chronic*. A growing number of other gangsta rappers have enjoyed platinum sales (over a million copies), such as Scarface (*The Diary*, Rap-A-Lot Records, 1994), and Bone Thugs and Harmony, whose album *E. 1999 Eternal* (Ruthless Records) entered the US pop charts at number one in August 1995.

As we have seen then, rap began as a simple form of street entertainment that improvized with the minimal tools of record turntables and microphones, and was gradually transformed into a multi-million dollar industry. Its lyrical themes moved from harmless street bravado to social commentary and 'conscious' black politics. And in 1995—at the peak of its popularity among whites and blacks—the rap scene has come to be dominated by records that concentrate on themes of violence.

There is no doubt that gangsta rap is popular today, but is it a valid artform? Various arguments are used to justify its existence by interested parties, but there is one that pre-dominates, namely, that violence, gang warfare, drugs, alcohol and casual sex are rife in the ghetto and therefore speaking about these subjects is a true reflection of 'reality'. This argument is put most succinctly by Ice Cube: 'We call ourselves underground street reporters. We just tell it how we see it, nothing more, nothing less.'[8] Scarface says of his violent rap: 'It should be taken as a story ... I'm not trying to scare, I'm trying to explain the reality of these situations. I use profanities because people do.'[9] And Jerry Heller, ex-manager of NWA, asserts: 'I firmly believe that NWA are audio documentarians [sic]. They tell a story that happens where they grew up, and is still happening where they grew up and live, that needs to be told. And they tell it in the first person, even though much of it is from a third-person perspective. It just happens to work better musically in the first person.'[10]

Are gangsta rappers merely 'street reporters', documentalists who are seeking earnestly to educate us to 'the reality of these situations'? Whether the true role of art is simply to reflect everyday reality is questionable,[11] but nevertheless let us suppose for a moment that this were the case. While few would deny that the themes of gangsta rap are everyday realities in the lives of many, its crudely articulated violent pictures represent only a single version or perspective of social reality. Critic Stanley Crouch says of this: 'You cannot make a powerful Afro-American culture if you're going to base it on what hustlers and pimps think about the world. Those people have a distorted, vulgar vision of life because they live in a criminal atmosphere in which they see people at their very worst.'[12] Black activist C. DeLores Tucker is likewise convinced that the music sends a message to the entire world that black people are subhuman.[13] And even pro-rap writer S. H. Fernando, Jr. concedes that '... [gangsta] rap may, indeed, reinforce certain ugly stereotypes and celebrate pathological behaviour...'[14]

Furthermore, the image of 'street reporters'—who by

definition must be impartial and objective—is weakened by the whole ethos of gangsta rap, which stipulates that the rapper must be authentic, 'real' and not 'fake'. As black film-maker Spike Lee says: 'In America, to be a platinum [million-selling] artist now you've gotta be charged with murder—you'll sell five million albums. Because you're "real". You're "down". You're "hardcore". If you're a rapper who ain't killed nobody or raped nobody [people think] "shit, I ain't buying that record".'[15] Indeed, in the context of this macho culture of being 'real', it is difficult to experience any dramatic distance or element of story-telling when, for example, rapper Scarface, 'screaming for vengeance', threatens to 'blow out your mother****ing brains'.[16]

But let us suppose for a moment that gangsta rap *is* a legitimate and true reflection of 'reality'. In reflecting this 'reality' does it educate, as purported above, or does it have a negative influence on its listeners and contribute to levels of violence in society? MC Eiht is forthright in his dismissal of the latter contention: 'Ain't no song in this mother****in' planet gonna make you go out and kill nobody.'[17] Bushwick Bill of the Geto Boys says: 'How the **** is my album gonna tell you to go out and kill people? It's something that was already within your heart to go out and do, and you just wanted a good excuse.'[18] Similarly, Snoop Doggy Dogg reacts negatively to the point: 'They bring out that I'm a gangsta rapper promoting violence. How the **** am I promoting violence when it was goin' on before I was born?'[19]

Few people would contend, of course, that gangsta rap or any other artform is the original creator of violence, or is solely responsible for society's ills. Many blacks, perhaps understandably, see the focus of attack on phenomena like gangsta rap as a diversion from the actual root causes of modern social problems of crime, poverty, unemployment and so on. However, it would be wrong to be content with this thought; for the question we should ask in this case is whether gangsta rap adds to the general *atmosphere* of violence in society. In this sense, in an indirect way, it might be a pernicious contributory factor to social problems. Certainly, as psychologist Na'im Akbar—a former president of the Association of Black Psychologists—points out: 'You can't prove that it [gangsta rap] is causative, but it's certainly correlational.'[20] And indeed 'black-on-black' violence has escalated sharply since the late 1980s (when gangsta rap began gaining popularity) while the number of juveniles arrested for murder increased by more than 50 per cent from 1988 to 1992, with juvenile arrests for violent crime increasing at almost the same rate.[21]

Ronald Ray Howard, who was sentenced to death in Texas by a jury in July 1993 for the murder of a highway patrolman, attempted in his defence to make a direct link between gangsta rap and his own violent actions. Howard, who was listening to Tupac Shakur's *2PACALYPSE NOW* while driving in his car, is reported to have said: 'The music was up as loud as it could go with gunshots and siren noises on it and my heart was pounding hard. I watched him [the patrolman] get out of his car in my side view mirror, and I was so hyped up, I just snapped. I jacked a bullet in the chamber and when he was close enough, I turned around and bam! I shot him.'[22] A lawyer for Time Warner (part-owners of Interscope Records who released *2PACALYPSE NOW*) stated in his company's defence: 'Unfortunately, the focus in the press has not been on the evil conduct of a career criminal, who appears to be a classic sociopath, but on the music he listened to. It was not a song that killed this fine officer but a bullet.'[23] Of course that is true, but it does not prove that the violent music did not act as a contributory factor.

Despite all the above difficulties with the genre, it is a fact that countless rappers have turned their backs on constructive and positive types of rap and jumped on the gangsta bandwagon. Why? C. DeLores Tucker, an antagonist of the 'reality' argument, gives an important indication, pointing to economic enticements: 'We can't say that they [gangsta rappers] are just speaking of reality. The reality is that they don't hate their own people; they are paid to say that. So many of them have said that it's the money. *The money*.'[24] Indeed rapper Dr Dre, speaking in an issue of *The Source* in 1990, was quite open about his interests in this regard: 'Bottom line: we ain't doing this shit to send out no messages, **** all that, we in this shit to get paid.'[25] Snoop Doggy Dogg also betrays this 'bottom line' interest: 'I'm trying to sell records. I ain't trying to make nobody happy. I'm trying to sell records.'[26]

But why should this type of rap be so popular with music buyers that it offers such great incentives to its creators? Snoop Doggy Dogg goes some way to answering this question, suggesting why gangsta rap exercises such a strong fascination on the majority white market: 'Because it's like a movie to them. It's a situation that they've never been in, but they're interested to know the mystery behind why blacks kill blacks, why there's gang violence, why there's drug peddling going on. It's just like a big movie to them...'[27] *Washington Post* feature writer David Mills makes the point more directly: 'Gangsta rap isn't about the reality of underclass America; it's about shock value. Show business. If these rappers were dedicated to "reality", how come they never deal with the results of the gunshots they throw into the mix.'[28]

If gangsta rap is just about show business—about thrilling its audience in the way that a horror film does—then one could only conclude that the exploitation of it by record companies is cynical. Lynne Cheney, a fellow of the American Enterprise Institute, subscribes to this view, suggesting that in backing gangsta rap record companies are 'polluting the culture' and that they should rather 'use their vast talents and resources to put us in touch with our best selves—instead of the worst part of our nature.'[29] But the record companies that promote gangsta rap are keen to counteract this objection by characterizing their critics as opponents of free speech and advocates of censorship. In this vein, Time Warner chairman Gerald Levin wrote in defence of his artist Ice T in the *Wall Street Journal*: 'The test of any democratic society lies not in how well it can control expression but in whether it gives freedom of thought and expression the widest possible latitude, however controversial or exasperating the results may sometimes be.' In a firm stand he added: 'We won't retreat in the face of threats of boycotts or political grandstanding.'[30]

This argument can be seen as a diversion. Of course, censorship cannot be a cure for political, social and spiritual problems—it is only a way of covering them up. But this supposed conviction in free speech is clearly not the reason why record companies have concentrated resources on gangsta rap. So why has it predominated and been promoted over other types of rap? This question is not only a concern of politicians and newspaper critics. Chuck D of Public Enemy—whose record *It Takes a Nation of Millions to Hold Us Back* was voted to be the finest rap record of all time in *Hip-Hop Connection* magazine—said in an interview: '...the record companies found it [gangsta rap] was a way to sell many, many records. Therefore their A&R [Artist & Repertory] departments pretty much kept the point of view one-sided.'[31] This opinion is backed up by gangsta rapper MC Eiht, speaking during a debate in which he defended gangsta rap. In a shrewd mimicking of record company executives, he says: '"Ain't no mother****in' way you gonna stop us makin' money off these niggers." And that's when you gonna get the president of Epic and Warner Brothers comin' to court.'[32]

In an earlier interview, Chuck D suggested action: 'You know, black kids shouldn't be pointing guns at each other; they should be pointing them at the record company presidents. Then you'll see the shit cease. Ain't that a trick!

You want to roll up to these record companies and tell 'em to stop getting behind this stuff and exploiting it. Because they feel like, "Hey! It ain't my community!" ' To the retort that the rappers themselves surely were also responsible, Chuck D answered: 'But they're young. In this business they're the youth, and they're only doing things to survive. The ones that are on top of them, paying them—they're the ones that are responsible.'[33]

How true is this accusation, that record companies have concentrated on gangsta rap because of its money-making potential? Writer Jim Shelly gives an important indication regarding this question, relating the significance of interest in rap by white people to the rise of gangsta rap. In the ghetto, he points out, rap is consumed 'through radio, home-made tapes, pirate copies, parties and clubs', whereas whites are much more likely to purchase compact discs and other official record company products. 'This has returned some of the collective control over rap to the big white corporations and marketing departments,' he adds.[34] A film that parodied rap, *CB4*, has a scene in which a worried record company executive asks his prospective gangsta rapper signings whether they 'defile women and cuss on your records? Do you fondle your genitalia on stage and glorify the use of guns?' When they say 'yes', he beams and shouts, 'Sign here.'

And yet it must be said that such exploitation, however cynical, is entirely within the bounds and rules of free-market capitalism. According to the economic laws of supply and demand, the record companies are providing products which people freely choose to purchase. That the companies might be seeking deliberately to appeal to 'the worst part of our nature' (in the words of Lynne Cheney) is, in the context of the amoral laws of the free market, irrelevant. Author and professor John Edgar Wideman with irony points out this contradiction in modern American social thinking: 'Let's deregulate everything; let the marketplace rule. Except when rap music captures a lion's share of the multi-billion dollar music market. Then, in the name of decency and family values, we're duty bound to regulate it.'[35]

Gangsta rappers and record companies, therefore, are working (in a somewhat unholy alliance) within the American traditions of free speech and free market capitalism. Given that the 'marketplace rules', it is understandable that such an economics will work to the lowest common denominator—taking advantage of people's base fascinations and lower desires. As writer Steven Daly concludes at the end of an interview with gangsta rapper Dr Dre: 'He's giving the people what they want: an amped-up mix of profane free speech, guns and sex. And making millions in the process—what could be more American than that?'[36]

*

In his ground-breaking work *The Spiritual Origins of Eastern Europe and the Future Mysteries of the Holy Grail*, the central chapters of which hold the key to understanding our present times, Sergei O. Prokofieff describes how certain secret 'brotherhoods' of the West work against the true evolution of humanity by 'the widest possible dissemination of every kind of materialism'.[37] Through occult means, members of such groups strive to 'gain the possibility of having an influence upon earthly events also after their death and, hence, of *occultly* intensifying earthly materialism from the sphere bordering upon the Earth.'[38] Such measures assist their intention to 'super-materialize' materialism.

These brotherhoods, Prokofieff continues, develop their malign influences through modern materialistic science and the inappropriate use of technology. However, they also work through popular culture, aiding the destruction of fledgling spiritual capacities through encouraging 'with the help of financial and other sources of support ... manifestations of disintegration and decadence'. Their chief aim is the eventual materialization of the consciousness soul 'so that it would be impossible for it to receive the Spirit Self in the sixth epoch'.[39]

Such ideas may seem unfounded and somewhat fantastic. How, after all, do such degenerating influences work on a practical level? Of course such occult brotherhoods must be, by definition, truly hidden, and hence it is not possible to speak of them directly. We can also assume that in their ambitions to remain secret they strive to blind humanity to their methods. Rudolf Steiner, however, in his bid to awaken mankind to the malevolent goals of such brotherhoods, hoped that people would be able to develop clear thinking and a discriminating faculty that would enable them to perceive how certain materializing tendencies are developed and encouraged—'with the help of financial and other sources of support', as Prokofieff states.

This brief survey of the story of rap has shown how basic economic imperatives, when allowed to run their course through the 'free market', conspire to deliver a degenerating culture as their 'product'. Such an outcome is almost inevitable within the modern economic system as better financial returns are, in general, achieved from products that appeal to people's lower instincts. In the case of rap music we have seen how a potentially fruitful form was snatched up by corporations that encouraged its most violent and ugly manifestation in their hunger for profit. The eventual triumph of the sub-genre of gangsta rap, which in its alluring titillation of human beings' lower selves offered the widest appeal, was a process determined, therefore, by the economic system.

As Rudolf Steiner has shown, a true harmony between the three spheres of culture, economics and politics can only be found when they are allowed to flourish independently of each other.[40] Relating the slogan of the French Revolution—'freedom, equality and fraternity'—to culture, politics and economics respectively, he suggested that we should apply a different thinking to each area of social life. Thus, cultural life should be 'free', individual political rights 'equal', and economics based on 'fraternity'. Once we muddle our thinking and misapply these concepts, or allow the three spheres to become entangled and subservient to each other, we are in danger of creating social chaos.

In the emergence of gangsta rap we see a complete subjugation of the cultural life (music in this case) to the economic life (the record companies and their market). Reacting to this situation, one could—like Bob Dole—castigate the record companies for cultivating 'moral confusion for profit' or blame the gangsta rappers for selling their souls, but that would not be dealing with the actual cause of the problem. For the pernicious rise of gangsta rap is due, ultimately, to the structure of the social system.

As Prokofieff asserts, the goal of certain western brotherhoods is the 'super-materialization' of materialism. In the current context we can see this 'super-materialism' in the gross distortion of American culture (a caricature which Rudolf Steiner referred to as 'Americanism') which, based on the repression of culture by economics, is responsible for developing phenomena like gangsta rap. It is not surprising that a spiritual archetype for social life (such as we find in Anthroposophy) will not be welcomed by the retrogressive forces that produce the stifling atmosphere of super-materialism.

To research and observe truly the work of the *occult* brotherhoods on the occult level to which Rudolf Steiner was able, one would need to develop a high level of clairvoyance. Other investigators in this field have acquired a genuine detective ability to apprehend shadowy figures and consciously participating conspirators, while the vast majority of writers on this subject have built illusory, fantastic models and theories. However, through ordinary human faculties we can all perceive certain methods that such groups employ to permeate culture with materialism. For, as we have seen, it is the social structure of the West, which is venerated and defended with detailed and elaborate arguments, that is responsible for promoting decadent culture like gangsta rap. And it is through the dissemination of such social ideas—spreading now throughout eastern Europe and the world—that the occult brotherhoods of the West are able to spread their supermaterial 'Americanism'.

It is a natural response to experience helplessness and despair when one perceives the entrenched might of such forces, but such feelings can only fuel their power. On the other hand, clear thinking which can approach a true perception of reality is, in its spiritual power, already a force for the good and a preparation for the future.

5
THE CASE OF DAVID ICKE

Modern Manifestations of Evil

In March 1991 David Icke gave written notice of his immediate resignation as national spokesman of the Green Party in Britain. He warned that the imminent publication of his book would put him 'at the centre of tremendous controversy'.[1] A few days later Icke held a press conference to publicize his recently acquired spiritual convictions. The media reaction to his pronouncements was dramatic. Icke was vilified and denounced as a madman who believed he was 'the Son of God'.

David Icke began his career as a professional goalkeeper with the English team Coventry City. On developing arthritis he was forced to give up football at the age of 21, and gradually established himself as a successful sports journalist and television presenter. As Icke approached the end of his thirties, he began to take an interest in environmental issues and joined the Green Party. In February 1990 he had a booklet published, *It Doesn't Have to Be Like This*, in which he celebrated the Green Party as one which was 'not prepared to tell the people what they wanted to hear if that was at odds with the truth...'[2] Six months after joining the party he reached a prominent position in its collective leadership, travelling across Britain to further the Green cause, giving interviews and press conferences.

Icke's conversion to ecological and environmental politics led him to question the hegemonic materialistic conception of life: '...the deeper I travelled into Green politics, the more it became a spiritual journey. I was soon asking many questions about the reason for our existence. Why were we here? What happened next?'[3] His search took him to 'medium and healer' Betty Shine. Through this meeting Icke was introduced to spiritual ideas and was 'led to a stream of books', including those of Edgar Cayce. Later, Icke described this meeting with Betty Shine as a turning-point: 'Through Betty I received some astonishing revelations and predictions of fundamental importance to the future of humankind which set me on a journey of discovery that I would have found impossible to comprehend unless my path had crossed with hers.'[4]

As Icke's interest grew, he became convinced that he had an important role to play in helping to alert humanity to the spiritual foundations of its existence. The 'spiritual communications' he received led him to believe that, as a public figure, his task was to write and publish influential books which would awaken people to the dangers of materialism.

By March 1991, Icke's book *The Truth Vibrations* was completed, and scheduled for a May publication. Icke now decided to stage a press conference in London, in which he appeared on a platform with his wife, daughter, and follower Deborah Schawsun. All were uniformly dressed in turquoise tracksuits. Surrounded by cynical newsmen, Icke spoke at some length about the crisis facing humanity, warning of widespread natural disasters if things did not change. 'The biggest threat to the Earth is thought pollution,' he declared, adding, 'any imbalance filters up to God ... We can balance the Earth so the Earth will not be destroyed.'[5] He explained to his audience that such disasters as earthquakes, hurricanes and tidal waves occurred as a cleansing action by the Earth, which desired to 'rid itself of energies trapped by evil feelings of anger, hatred and aggression.'[6]

Icke also proclaimed: 'I channel an energy known as the Christ Spirit.'[7] He elucidated to the disbelieving spectators that 'Christ isn't a person, it's an energy known as pure love and wisdom and resonates to the same frequency as the colour turquoise.'[8]

The conference was a disaster for Icke, effectively killing his reputation as a respected minor celebrity. The tabloid newspapers gave wide coverage to the story, all maintaining that Icke had introduced himself as 'the Son of God'. *The Sun* asked its readers 'IS DAVID ICKE OFF HIS BIKE?', and quoted psychologist Glenn Wilson as saying: 'He's not mad, but his ideas are certainly crazy.'[9] The paper also held a telephone poll in which it enquired 'Do you think Icke has gone bonkers?' The results were published the following day—beneath a story headlined 'ICKE IS MY SON, NOT THE LORD'S SAYS MUM'—revealing that *Sun* readers had voted by more than 4–1 to affirm the charge that Icke had, indeed, 'gone bonkers'.

The Daily Mirror similarly showed little tolerance for Icke's new stand, heading its story as 'the Loony Gospel of Saint David' and quoting another psychologist, Gary Cooper, as claiming that Icke was probably going through a mid-life crisis. According to *The Daily Mirror*, only one man welcomed Icke's words, the chairman of the Raving Loony Green Giant party, Stuart Hughes, who reportedly enthused: 'He's the man for us.'[10]

The oft-repeated charge that Icke had 'declared himself the Son of God' was based on Icke's statement that he was a 'channel for the Christ spirit'. Although it was a misrepresentation, the 'Son of God' tag stuck, and led to a perception in the mass-consciousness that Icke simply was demented.

In his book *The Truth Vibrations* Icke describes how, with the aid of 'psychic and astrologer' Judy Hall, his previous incarnations had allegedly been traced—revealing him to have been most recently a 'soldier, spy and medium'. The 'spirit messages', which make up the core of *The Truth Vibrations*, refer to him as 'still a child spiritually'.[11] Nevertheless, he does assume the position of a prophet and an individuality endowed with a sacred mission:

My role would be to help bring about a spiritual revolution, and I would become a 'cosmic parent' to the planet and humanity[12] ... I had a job to do in this lifetime that would, in conjunction with other events and other people, change the world forever. I felt a bit isolated and lonely with the knowledge I had been given, but the Grand Plan was soon to take care of that.[13]

While far from being the work of a madman, *The Truth Vibrations* cannot be regarded as a profound esoteric study. *The Sunday Times* magazine described it, not altogether unfairly, as 'a belch of semi-digested spiritualist, New Age and mystic canons of belief'.[14] As a populist New Age discourse, it is not dissimilar in content to many dozens published each year. However, If we wish to examine the validity of *The Truth Vibrations* further, our primary consideration—as with the assessment of any spiritual research—should be the reliability of the methodology which is used. Icke admits that the esoteric substance of his book is not the product of his own research. His information is mostly gathered from 'spirit messages' conveyed through individuals whose techniques centre on automatic writing, mediumship and 'channelling'. The student of modern spiritual science has good reason to be wary of these means of investigation, all of which sacrifice the fully alert consciousness required of the modern initiate, leaving room for serious error in results and possible manipulation by occult sources.

Perhaps it is not surprising, therefore, that *The Truth Vibrations* contains many anomalies. Sometimes these are straightforward inaccuracies due to poor exoteric research. For example, the Grail cup is described as 'a chalice cup made from the cross on which Christ was crucified'.[15] However, with regard to Icke's esoteric disclosures we also find some questionable information of a more serious nature. In one instance Icke makes a list of the incarnations of a being described as 'Rakorczy, the Ascended Master, the Lord of Civilization and Lord of the Seventh Ray', which includes: '...a High Priest in Atlantis, Joseph (the father of Jesus), the prophet Samuel, Saint Alban, Merlin ... the monk scientist Roger Bacon, Christopher Columbus, the Count Saint-Germain of France, and Francis Bacon.'[16] An identical list of incarnations for Saint Germain is to be found in *Intermediate Studies in Alchemy*,[17] allegedly authored by Saint-Germain himself, and produced by the occult group based in California founded by Mark L. Prophet and Elizabeth Clare Prophet. However, based on his first-hand, highly-trained clairvoyant research, Rudolf Steiner identified Francis Bacon as the individuality who had incarnated earlier as Harun-al-Rashid.[18] The Count Saint-Germain was an incarnation of the great Christian initiate Christian Rosenkreutz,[19] and Merlin was an earlier incarnation of the composer Wagner.[20]

A further striking characteristic of Icke's work is his apparent materialization of the spiritual world. His preoccupation with changing 'vibrations', 'frequencies' and 'energies'—not uncommon in the New Age movement—may remind us of Rudolf Steiner's critique of the theosophist A. P. Sinnett's book *Esoteric Buddhism*. Steiner regarded Sinnett's claim that the Moon constituted the 'Eighth Sphere' as such a dangerous falsity that he devoted several lectures to correcting it.[21] His comments on Sinnett are pertinent to our reflections on David Icke:

> Sinnett was a journalist and was therefore steeped in the materialistic tendencies of the nineteenth century; here, then, was a personality whose brain tended entirely to materialism, but the longing for a spiritual world was also present in him. He therefore had every aptitude for seeking for the spiritual world in a materialistic form... Of course, the teaching about the members of man's being, the doctrine of karma and reincarnation, are

truths. But materialism has here been woven into all these truths. In Sinnett's *Esoteric Buddhism* a genuinely spiritual outlook is combined with an eminently materialistic tendency...[22]

While Icke seems to be unaware of the danger of such tendencies to creep into his spiritual writings, he does at least appreciate that 'communication between other planes and dimensions is not like picking up the telephone ... some of the sharpness of the message can be lost.' He also recognizes that 'some of what I have said in terms of detail I will modify in future books' and 'there is still an enormous amount I do not know'.[23] Nevertheless, from the standpoint of a modern *science* of the spirit, the dilettantism evident in the means of his research is not a trivial matter.

And yet, perversely, *The Truth Vibrations* (as with Sinnett's *Esoteric Buddhism*) does have much redeeming material. Among the mishmash of theosophical terminology and New Age vernacular, students of Anthroposophy may be surprised to discover material such as the following on reincarnation, which coincides with a Christian understanding of the teaching:

> There is no sense of retribution in karma. It is not the product of a vengeful God ... We are given the gift of free will to make our own decisions about which lives we shall have or if we will keep to our life-plan once we have incarnated ... but it is comforting to know that our souls, spirit guides and guardian angels are always trying to re-create the situations which will bring us back on course... The soul, often in consultation with spiritual teachers, selects the parents which will offer the best chance of providing the lessons it wishes to learn, and incarnates as their child ... When karmic debts are built up between certain souls, they must incarnate together to pay them back.[24]

He shows an understanding of the Akashic Record: 'In the spiritual world beyond our sight every thought and deed of every life-form is recorded on a fine substance known as the Akashic Records.'[25] And Icke even has a healthy, practical approach to the modern spiritual path: 'Not everything that calls itself "New Age" is desirable. Some of it is not. Walking around in a spiritual daze and ignoring the practical necessities of life on the physical plane is of little use to anyone. It is balance we are searching for.'[26]

In fact, it could be contended that there is sufficient material in his book to lead many people to a spiritual awakening, or at least provide a starting point for research. Moreover, the reader of *The Truth Vibrations* will find it difficult not to warm to Icke, whose honest enthusiasm is refreshing, and it would take a hardened cynic to claim that he is not sincere. In January 1992, following reports that he had renounced his previous work and had admitted 'madness', Icke struck back in a letter to *The Guardian* in which he affirmed that he would continue to 'expound the truths of reincarnation, karma, and the nature of the current transformation of humanity and the planet'. Icke concluded with characteristic vigour: 'Walking away? I haven't even started yet.'[27]

All this may leave us with ambivalent feelings and a confusing and seemingly contradictory picture. With the aid of Rudolf Steiner's research, however, we may tentatively discern some of the forces active behind Icke and his work.

The ahrimanic attack

Icke's words at his initial press conference amounted to an unexpected challenge to the materialistic supposition which underpins our society. His subsequent treatment by the press can be seen as a fierce reaction to this perceived

challenge. A study of the language used to describe Icke—
'loony', 'bonkers', 'off his bike'—reveals familiar dismissive
tactics employed in such circumstances. In particular, the
use by the media of the highly emotive term 'Son of God'
may be considered as an insidious and underhand strategy
to undermine everything he had said. And it was not just
the tabloid papers that adopted such methods to dispose of
Icke's arguments. *The Sunday Times* magazine devoted
several pages to analysing Icke's life and times in an
endeavour to depict him as a psychologically unstable and
power-hungry megalomaniac, concluding that: 'He has
ostentatiously renounced the entire network of consensus
and order of concessions by which a society agrees to conduct its business and to regulate its arguments.'[28]

In reflecting on such reactions one need not think in terms
of a conscious media conspiracy against the spirit; rather, a
clue to explaining such attacks is given by Rudolf Steiner in
his 'karma lectures' of 1924, where he explicitly warned
that, increasingly during the course of the twentieth century, Ahriman would work as an author through the
manipulation of human individuals. He further cautioned
that 'Ahriman will write his works in the strangest places—
but they will be there indeed—and he is preparing pupils
for his purposes... In every sphere watchfulness will be
needed.'[29]

Our 'watchfulness' may not be sufficient if we search for
Ahriman's authorship only in scientific journals and scho-
larly and academic works. In his attempt to govern the
human being, Ahriman will be working to divert mankind's attention from the spiritual through every channel
open to him. Therefore the spiritual battle today will be
waged as vehemently against the vast masses of ordinary
people as it is in universities and colleges.

This may throw some further light on why the media
attacked Icke with such fervour. As an ex-footballer and
television presenter he was a popular public figure from the

'cultural mainstream' of society. His celebrity status meant that he would be listened to by ordinary people and be given wide access to modern means of communication—thus being able to spread his message to those who would not normally come into contact with such ideas.

In this regard Icke has already proved that, when given the opportunity, he has the charisma and style to convince ordinary people of his point of view. In December 1991, for example, during an appearance on Channel 4 television's *Jonathan Ross Show*, he was initially roundly jeered and taunted by the studio audience on account of his 'loony' reputation. Undaunted, Icke responded with equanimity and assurance, accepting that he had made errors in his presentation since his initial public declaration. He went on to speak of the 'growing evidence around the world' of the truths of reincarnation and karma. After his brief appearance, Icke left the studio to loud cheers and applause.

The luciferic deception

It is a well-known occult maxim that a half-truth is more dangerous than a lie, as a lie is easier to detect and expose. In Icke's descriptions of the spiritual world and spiritual beings, especially his understanding of Christ, we may perceive subtle (and occasionally blatant) distortions of Christian-Rosicrucian teachings as we find them, in their most modern form, in anthroposophical spiritual science. Here, then, we are led to question where Icke's information originates from.

As has been said, it is particularly his commentaries on Christ which act as pointers to the possible source of Icke's 'spiritual communications'. Although he speaks of the Christ Spirit as 'an aspect of the Solar Logos', ultimately Icke perceives Christ only as a master with a teaching which 'had a positive effect on humanity in that it highlighted the

values of compassion, peace and love for all things'.[30] The
essential nature of the Mystery of Golgotha remains
unknown to him. For example, he demonstrates a fundamental misunderstanding of Christ's deed for humanity in
the following statement:

> He [Christ] could have responded to the prospect of
> death on the cross by unleashing his immense power
> against the forces of darkness, but such an occult battle
> would have caused so much damage to the Earth and its
> people that he decided to go quietly to his physical death.
> In this sense, you could say that Jesus died to save us
> all.[31]

From his own occult research, however, Rudolf Steiner
confirmed the basic truth which lies behind the traditional
Christian concept of Redemption. Through the influence of
Lucifer in Lemurian times, mankind was plunged prema-
turely into matter:

> Through the luciferic event man gained a great benefit: he
> became a free being. But he also incurred a liability: the
> propensity to deviate from the path of the good and the
> right, and from the path of the true. What has happened
> in the course of incarnations is a matter of karma. But all
> that has crept down from the macrocosm into the
> microcosm, all that the luciferic forces have given to man,
> is something that man cannot deal with by himself. To
> compensate for the objective luciferic event, another
> objective act was needed ... One cannot by any means
> treat the luciferic influence as an objective act without
> treating in the same manner the compensating act, the
> Event of Golgotha.[32]

This compensating act of sacrifice, of the Redemption of
'original sin', is—in all its esoteric significance—seriously
misunderstood in Icke's work.

We have already concluded that the methods of spiritual

research used in providing material for *The Truth Vibrations*—mediumship, channelling, automatic writing—give open access to influences from a range of spiritual sources, yet Icke repeatedly exhibits a complete faith in the accuracy of his findings: 'All the information in these pages has come through psychic communications or been confirmed as accurate by those communications.'[33] '...[T]he vast majority of what you have read and are about to read is absolutely correct.'[34] His reliance on 'channelling' is of particular concern: 'To channel is to allow a spirit to speak through you. The spirit puts thought forms into the mind, and the channel turns them into words and speaks them.'[35] However, as has been indicated earlier, without the ability to verify the nature of such an influence through a highly developed and discriminating clairvoyance, one is at the mercy of those who may wish to present a subjective and coloured occultism.

Let us return once more to Rudolf Steiner's comments on A. P. Sinnett's *Esoteric Buddhism*. Steiner claimed that 'Sinnett wrote it [the book]—but behind him was the one he calls his inspirer, and whom we know as the later mask of a Mahatma-individuality.'[36] When, in his notes to Edouard Schuré, Steiner described the present tendency of eastern initiation and the Mahatmas who stand behind it, he stated that: '...the eastern initiations must of necessity leave untouched the Christ as the central cosmic factor of evolution... They could only hope for success within evolution if the principle of Christianity were to be eradicated from western culture.'[37] Steiner stressed that a Christ-orientated esotericism is now essential for the 'meaning and destiny of the Earth'.[38]

From the above we are given an intimation as to the possible true nature of the beings which are given the names 'Rakorczy' and 'Attarro', referred to frequently by Icke as the source of the 'communications'. In his approach to Christianity we may further assume that the true origin

of these sources is retrogressive and inspired from a luciferic realm relating to the old eastern initiation. Certainly, in
his reliance on methods more suited to past epochs, a tendency towards such inspiration is manifested by Icke.

Further, if we study as objectively as possible Icke's own
personal behaviour at the time of the writing of his first
book, an empowerment by such forces of a luciferic nature
becomes evident—particularly during the initial emergence
of his spiritual revelations. Here we see personal delusion
working especially strongly, notably in his public asser-
tion—and absolute conviction—that he channelled the
Christ Spirit. We see it also in the statements (referring to
himself) such as: 'One man cannot change the world, but
one man can communicate the message that can change the
world.'[39]

From his own biographical account it is plain that Icke
undertook his mission without sufficient inner preparation
or esoteric training. He was thus especially perceptible to
deceptions and delusions. Unfortunately he was quite
unaware of his own shortcomings in this respect: 'I have
been left in no doubt whatsoever about the scale of oppo-
sition I will face. I knew that when I began, and am prepared for whatever may come.'[40]

From our reflections a picture gradually emerges of an
earnest figure with integrity who is, however, unwittingly
pulled from two directions. From one side we see ahrimanic
forces—which seek to drag humanity into cold materialism
in their desperation to eliminate any mention of the spirit—
working to influence mass culture through the media. And
from the other side we see luciferic forces—which seek to
draw humanity into a spiritual fantasy by attempting to
present a contorted picture of the spiritual world—hauling
Icke into an inflated self-importance.

In the experiences of David Icke, therefore, the dual
adversary forces may be apprehended in their attempts to
disrupt the delicate destiny of mankind. In recognizing the

working of these forces, we can come to a non-judgemental understanding of this period of Icke's life, and through viewing his experience we can awaken to the complexities of the modern path we are faced with as human beings. For, as Icke himself points out:

> It is not an environmental crisis that we have first and foremost, nor a crisis of injustice, nor of peace, nor of cruelty. They are the by-products of the real crisis that faces us—the crisis of the human spirit. We will only solve those ills if we remove the cause of them, and the cause is that the spiritual truths that hold all the answers have been lost.[41]

6

THE QUESTION OF RACE, I

Malcolm X and the Michael Impulse

Race in the USA

On 3 March 1991 Rodney King, an unemployed labourer on parole for robbery, was kicked and beaten with batons by three members of the Los Angeles Police Department for over two minutes while 11 other policemen looked on. *The Times* reported that his injuries included 'nine skull fractures, a broken leg, concussion, a shattered eye socket, damage to his knees, and partial paralysis of his face'.[1] King's car had been chased by police officers after a California highway patrol car team had reported that it was speeding.

The beating incident was secretly filmed by a bystander trying out his new video camera, and the resulting dramatic film was soon seen by television viewers all over the world. It was noted that Rodney King was black and the police officers white. Minority groups asserted that the beating differed from many others only in that a camera was present. The Los Angeles chief of police, Daryl Gates, played down the incident as 'an aberration' and refused to resign. Following the beating, Rodney King was jailed for three days before being released without any charges.

Just over a year later a jury acquitted the policemen of all charges, despite the graphic evidence of the video tape. The response from elements of the black community in the United States was immediate and violent, with rioting and looting in many cities—particularly Los Angeles where at least 44 people were killed and over 5,500 arrested. Once again, television pictures of these events were immediately flashed around the world.

Following the riots, in a special edition of *The Oprah Winfrey Show* entitled 'LA Talks Back', a young black man exclaimed angrily: 'I'm looking at the news and they are telling me my life is not worth a nickel. They are telling me they can beat me, they can do whatever they want to me whenever they feel like it.'

These episodes did little to alleviate the chronic racial tensions within American society, where the dream of the racial 'melting-pot' appears to have been usurped by a growing consciousness of ancestry and ethnic identity. Alongside this trend, a polarization between blacks and whites is also evident. This divide is aggravated by the difficult social position of many African-Americans. Despite the growth of a black middle class, which is gradually gaining political strength and cultural influence, a large portion of the black community lives in poor social conditions ravaged by violence, drugs and crime.[2]

In recent years, the highly addictive cocaine-derivative 'crack' has been a catalyst in the critical problems of American inner cities. Crack, which is said to provide the most intense 'high' of any known drug, has a brief effect and leaves the user desperate for the money to pay for the next 'hit', thus contributing to violent crime. A concentration of the underprivileged in housing 'projects' helps to create ghettos, with few 'role models' for the youth to emulate—while black unemployment runs far above the national average. On the west coast 'gangbanging'—armed gangs battling for drug territory—is a formidable problem, with the scourge of 'driveby shootings' an everyday reality in some communities.

A reaction by some African-Americans to this desperate plight has been to emphasize the positive characteristics of their people. Such attributes are labelled 'Afrocentric' as opposed to 'Eurocentric'. A view along these lines is expressed by Professor Leonard Jeffries of the Department of Black Studies, New York City College: 'The European has proved his bankruptcy. He's polluting the seas, he's polluting the air, he's damaged the ozone layers, North and South Pole... Because of the European's value system of materialism and greed, based around the so-called market economy, African people, with their value system of caring and sharing, have to move to the head of ... the United States.'[3] Another example of a call for a regenerated Afrocentric culture comes from leading '60s black activist Sonny Carson: 'We are going to hear Malcolm [X] again, right through these young people [saying] ... "we are a new people seeking a new order and we are going to get it by any means necessary."'[4]

The popular music form known as rap or hip-hop is at present the chief vehicle for the expression of the opinions of African-American youth.[5] (The lead vocalist of the group Public Enemy referred to rap as 'the CNN [Cable News Network] of black America'.) Over the years, the lyrical content of various rap artists' recordings has become more explicit and extreme, and is sometimes used as a vent against the perceived white oppressor. References to the view that American blacks are victims of a genocidal conspiracy, which involves infesting their neighbourhoods with liquor and gun shops, allowing free availability of the drug crack and introducing the AIDS virus as a form of biological warfare, are not uncommon. On a recent release, for example, Ice Cube declares: '... to us [blacks] Uncle Sam is Hitler without ovens / Burning our black skin / Form the neighbourhood and then push the crack in / Doing us wrong from the first day / And don't understand why a nigger got an AK[47].' Further on he remarks acidly: 'The KKK [Ku-Klux-Klan] has got three-piece suits / Using niggers like turkey shoots.'[6] On another track he alludes to the acquittal of the policemen who beat Rodney King:

'...devils beat up a motorist, and get nothing but a slap on the wrist.'[7]

The frantic solution is to react with violence—to 'deal with the devil [the white man] with the mother****ing steel'. New York group Da Lench Mob gives a similar analysis, and also fantasize bloody revenge: 'Shoot you with my '22 / I got plenty crew to take out white boys, that's scary / Yea I'm the nigger that said it / and I'm sorry that I don't regret it / But it's a proven fact that Jack [the white man] is anti-black, so here's the ****ing payback.'*[8] Of the police, the Californian band NWA (Niggers with Attitude) claim: '...they don't want peace / They want a nigger to decease, so he'll cease to be a problem / And by the way they perform, I see the Klan gave the white police another uniform.' Their reaction is to go '...shooting everything in sight, tonight's the night / To get hype and fight for what's wrong, **** what's right'.[9]

This new militancy, almost nihilistic in its recklessness, contrasts strikingly with the American Civil Rights movement of the 1960s, which looked to the pacifist leadership of the Christian Martin Luther King. The hero of the present younger generation, which is living some 28 years after the height of the Civil Rights movement, is more likely to be the Muslim Malcolm X. In the tradition of the latter, freedom is a right to be won 'by any means necessary'. Linked with this attitude is a stress on affirming African identity, rather than seeking integration with white society.

The resurgence of interest in Malcolm X resulted in the young black director Spike Lee's film biography, released in 1992. Lee's film, arresting and confrontational, includes clips of the beating of Rodney King in an effort to show the current relevance of Malcolm X's cause. Based on Malcolm

---

* In relation to the development of rap described in Chapter 4, this type of violent 'anti-white' rap represents a 'gangsterization' of the pro-black (but non-violent) 'conscious' rap referred to there.

X's autobiography,[10] the film successfully portrays the life of a complex individual with a remarkable destiny.

The life path of Malcolm X

Malcolm X was born Malcolm Little in Omaha in 1925. One of his earliest memories was of his family's home being burnt down by a white supremacist group, the Black Legion. His father, a Baptist preacher who followed the 'back to Africa' teachings of Marcus Garvey, was killed two years later, allegedly by the same group. His mother, a Seventh Day Adventist, struggled to raise her children in conditions of poverty, but was declared insane and committed to a state mental hospital in 1939. The young Malcolm was placed in a juvenile home, moving later to various foster homes.

Leaving school early, Malcolm made his way to New York where he worked as a waiter in Harlem. He soon became involved in 'hustling', selling drugs and bootleg whiskey, and became addicted to cocaine. In 1946, following involvement in a string of thefts, he was arrested on charges of larceny, breaking and entering, and possession of firearms; he was sentenced to 10 years' imprisonment. While in prison he was introduced to the teachings of Elijah Muhammad, the leader of a Muslim sect named the Nation of Islam. The Honourable Elijah Muhammad, he was told, was 'the Messenger of Allah'. In 1931 Elijah Muhammad had apparently met 'God in person'[11] in the form of a Mr Wallace D. Fard. Fard had identified himself to Elijah Muhammad as 'a brother from the East' who had been born into the Koreish tribe of Muhammad ibn Abdulla.

Fard claimed to work with both the Koran and the Bible. He taught that the black people of America were 'the Lost-found Nation of Islam'. The first human beings on Earth— 'Original Man'—emerged on the continent of Africa and were black. They 'built great empires and civilizations and cultures while the white man was still living on all fours in caves'. The 'devil white man ... had pillaged, murdered, raped, and exploited every race of man not white'.[12]

> Human history's greatest crime was the traffic in black flesh when the devil white man went into Africa and murdered and kidnapped to bring to the West in chains, in slave ships, millions of black men, women and children, who were worked and beaten and tortured as slaves. The devil white man cut these black people off from all knowledge of their own kind, and cut them off from any knowledge of their own language, religion, and past culture, until the black man in America was the Earth's only race of people who had absolutely no knowledge of his true identity.[13]

According to Elijah Muhammad, the Christian religion, 'the white man's religion', taught the Negro to hate his colour, but to believe that 'everything white was good'. It further brainwashed 'the so-called Negro' to 'always turn the other cheek, and grin, and scrape, and bow, and be humble, and to sing, and to pray and to take whatever was dished out by the devilish white man; and to look for his pie in the sky, and for his heaven in the hereafter, while right here on earth the slavemaster white man enjoyed *his* heaven'.[14]

On this point, the Nation of Islam instruction is clear: 'No heaven was in the sky, Mr Fard taught, and no hell was in the ground. Instead both heaven and hell were conditions in which people lived right here on this planet Earth ... Also on Earth was the devil—the white race which was bred from black Original Man six thousand years before, purposely to create a hell on Earth for the next six thousand years.'[15] 'The black people, God's children, were Gods themselves ... And he taught that among them was one, also a human being like the others, who was the God of

Gods: the Most, Most High, the Supreme Being, supreme in wisdom and power—and His proper name was Allah.'[16]

Near the Last Day, or the End of Time, God would come to resurrect the Lost Sheep and separate them from their enemies. 'Master Fard taught that Prophecy referred to this Finder and Saviour of the Lost Sheep as the Son of Man, or God in Person, or the Lifegiver, the Redeemer, or the Messiah, who would come as lightning from the East and appear in the West. He was the One to whom the Jews referred to as the Messiah, the Christians as the Christ, and the Muslims as the Mahdi.'[17] According to Elijah Muhammad, the Master W. D. Fard represented the fulfilment of this prophecy. Mr Muhammad had asked Fard: ' "Who are you, and what is your real name?" He said, "I am the One the world has been looking for to come for the past two thousand years." I said to him again, "What is your name?" He said, "My name is Mahdi; I am God, I came to guide you into the right path..." '[18]

To the young Malcolm X in prison, this teaching had a potent effect. Although he was later to accuse Elijah Muhammad of 'religious fakery', Malcolm X admits in his autobiography that at the time he felt something close to St Paul's experience on the road to Damascus. His conversion to the Nation of Islam was swift, coinciding with a move to an experimental liberal reformatory. Here he began an intensive self-education with the help of the prison's extensive library.

> Book after book showed me how the white man had brought upon the world's black, brown, red and yellow peoples every variety of the sufferings of exploitation ... I read, I saw, how the white man never has gone among the non-white peoples bearing the Cross in the true manner and spirit of Christ's teachings—meek, humble, and Christlike. I perceived, as I read, how the collective white man had been actually nothing but a piratical

opportunist who used Faustian machinations to make his own Christianity his initial wedge in criminal conquests. First, always 'religiously', he branded 'heathen' and 'pagan' labels upon ancient non-white cultures and civilizations. The stage thus set, he then turned upon his non-white victims his weapons of war.[19]

In 1952 Malcolm X was let out on parole and immediately became closely involved with the Nation of Islam. He changed his surname from 'Little' to 'X' in a symbolic gesture to represent the loss of the African-American's heritage and culture. Malcolm X was soon appointed as a minister for the Nation of Islam, and rapidly ascended to the number two position in the organization. Through appearing on television shows such as *The Hate that Hate Produced*, he was almost singlehandedly responsible for raising the profile of the Nation of Islam around the world. A fiery, articulate and convincing speaker, Malcolm X won respect among whites, despite the radical opinions he expressed.

The Nation of Islam, an autocratic organization, expected extreme discipline from its adherents. The use of tobacco, alcohol, narcotics, and certain foods such as pork, were strictly proscribed. Fornication, dancing, gambling, film-going, sports, or even long holidays from work, were absolutely forbidden. The 'Black Muslims', as they came to be called, were expected to sleep 'no more than health required', to be courteous, lead a harmonious domestic life, and be honest and truthful. Life in the 'Temples' of the Nation was regimented, with different classes, trainings, lectures, discussion and services held each evening.

At the core of the Nation of Islam was a political pro-gramme which instructed that blacks should separate themselves from white society. The programme included a demand 'to be allowed to establish a separate state or ter-ritory', and called for the prohibition of intermarriage between races. In the meantime African-Americans should be exempt from all taxation 'as long as we are deprived of equal justice under the laws of the land'.[20] As Malcolm X recalls, Elijah Muhammad instructed that '... since western society is deteriorating, it has become overrun with immorality, and God is going to judge it, and destroy it. And the only way the black people caught up in this society can be saved is not to *integrate* into this corrupt society, but to *separate* from it, to a land of our *own* where we can reform ourselves, lift up our moral standards, and try to be godly.'[21]

In 1963, *The New York Times* reported that Malcolm X was the second most popular speaker in colleges and universities across the United States. He began to command as much admiration in academic circles as he did on the street in rallies and demonstrations. From December of that year, however, he was to be suspended from ministry and 'silenced' by Elijah Muhammad, apparently for remarks made about the assassination of John F. Kennedy. Following this decision, the relationship with Elijah Muhammad became strained, and on 8 March 1964 Malcolm X announced his break from the Nation of Islam and formed his own 'Muslim Mosque Inc.' in New York. Two months later, he embarked on travels to Mecca and Africa which were to change his life.

His pilgrimage to Mecca brought him for the first time into close proximity with mainstream Muslims. Malcolm X was overwhelmed by their natural hospitality and brotherhood. 'All ate as One, and slept as One. Everything about the pilgrimage atmosphere accented the Oneness of man under one God,' he recalled.[22] He also met white Muslims who extended the same warmth and friendliness towards him as he had experienced from members of his own race. 'The brotherhood! The people of all races, colours from all over the world coming together as one! It has proved to me the power of the One God.' He also felt, contrary to his previous separatist convictions, that '... the earth's most explosive and pernicious evil is racism, the inability of God's creatures to live as One, especially in the western world.'[23]

He wrote home to friends and family:

> For the past week, I have been utterly speechless and spellbound by the graciousness I see displayed all around me by people of all colours. But on this pilgrimage, what I have seen, and experienced, has forced me to rearrange much of my thought-patterns previously held, and to toss aside some of my previous conclusions ... I have been always a man who tries to face facts, and to accept the reality of life as new experience and new knowledge unfolds it. I have always kept an open mind, which is necessary to the flexibility that must go hand in hand with every form of intelligent search for truth.[24]

His letter was signed El-Hajj Malik El-Shabazz, his newly acquired Muslim name.

Malcolm X now began a complete reassessment of his previous ideology. 'In the past, yes, I have made sweeping indictments of all white people. I never will be guilty of that again—as I know now that some white people are truly sincere, that some truly are capable of being brotherly toward a black man.'[25] Back in America, while in his car at traffic lights, a man called over to him, 'Malcolm X, do you mind shaking hands with a white man?' to which he replied: 'I don't mind shaking hands with human beings. Are you one?'[26]

While Malcolm X continued campaigning uncompromisingly for the black man's cause, establishing the Organization of Afro-American Unity, his philosophy was now more open: 'I'm for truth, no matter who tells it. I'm for justice, no matter who it is for or against. I'm a human being first and foremost, and as such I'm for whoever and whatever benefits humanity *as a whole*.'[27] He also began

drawing deeply on his spiritual and religious understanding: 'Mankind's history has proved from one era to
another that the true criterion of leadership is spiritual. Men
are attracted by spirit. By power, men are forced. Love is
engendered by spirit. By power anxieties are created ... no
government laws ever can force brotherhood.'[28] His
analysis turned strongly against the political system, leading him to conclude that: '... the white man is not inherently
evil, but America's racist society influences him to act
evilly. The society has produced and nourishes a psychology which brings out the lowest, most base part of human
beings.'[29]

On 21 February 1965 Malcolm X was assassinated as he
began speaking at a public lecture. He died from several
gunshot wounds. He had been prophesying his own death
for months, indicating that the Nation of Islam could not
tolerate his continued teaching outside of their group.
However, the mystery of his death has never been fully
explained. Alex Haley (who was later to write the pheno-
menally popular slavery epic *Roots*) recalls that near the end
of his life Malcolm X became convinced that other agencies
apart from the Nation of Islam were involved in the
harassment he was experiencing. 'Things have happened
since that are bigger than what they can do. I know what
they can do. Things have gone beyond that.'[30] Alex Haley
also recounts that the police would not take Malcolm X's
requests for protection seriously. Although 20 policemen
had apparently been assigned to the meeting where he was
killed, and even agents of the Bureau of Special Services
were in attendance, '... these men were nowhere in evidence during or after the assassination...'[31]

In the months before Malcolm X's assassination, Alex
Haley had visited 'a very high government official' who
was interested in Malcolm X. Haley also records that when
Malcolm X arrived at the airport from his visit to Africa,
'... white men with cameras were positioned on the second

level, taking pictures of all the Negroes who entered, and almost as obvious were Negro plainclothesmen moving about.'[32]

Whoever was responsible for Malcolm X's murder— whether the Nation of Islam, a government agency, or a more secret organization—there is little doubt that the cause of their irritation was the evolution of his thinking. Malcolm X himself felt frustrated that the development of his ideas could not be accepted by either liberals or extremists: 'They won't let me turn the corner!' he exclaimed exasperated to Haley, 'I'm caught in a trap!'[33] To the end, however, he remained courageously open to new concepts. Shortly before his death he remarked to a reporter: 'I'm man enough to tell you that I can't put my finger on exactly what my philosophy is now, but I'm flexible.'[34]

In the early part of this century, Rudolf Steiner often spoke of the impulse brought from the spiritual worlds by the being who became the Time Spirit from 1879—previously the Archangel Michael. It was Michael's task, while still an Archangel, to 'conquer the dragon'. This conquering of the dragon by Michael meant that: 'Certain spiritual beings whose task in the spiritual world it was to divide mankind into races and peoples were cast out of Heaven down upon the Earth. These spiritual beings who up to the forties [of the nineteenth century] produced these differentiations among mankind have no longer any power in the region bordering the earthly world. They have been cast down among men upon the Earth with everything they could bring with them.'[35]

However, despite these hindering forces—'chiefly spirits of falsehood'—now present among mankind, it is the task 'for those who may be said to be of good will' to fight for the true spirituality of our times. 'It is not a tendency of the spiritual worlds to create further differences among mankind, but it is a tendency of the spiritual worlds to pour a cosmopolitan element over mankind.'[36] Further, '...clair-voyant vision shows that it was the spirit who was to become the Time Spirit of the modern age [Michael] that from the forties onwards fought against the race spirits, the folk spirits that produced the difference between peoples.' The true character of a 'Michael Age', therefore, is a cos-mopolitan, spiritualized culture.

It is not difficult to perceive these 'spirits of falsehood' working within the violent racial tensions and hatred described above. On the other hand, within his lifetime, Malcolm X was able to metamorphose his prejudices into a tolerant philosophical and spiritual questioning. Although when it came to Christianity he could not differentiate between its true spiritual essence and the historical crimes committed in its name, and was thus denied an objective, conscious recognition of the being of Christ, his finding of 'true Islam' towards the end of his life enabled him to enter upon a path of spiritual discovery which led him to sup-port, in his own words, 'whatever benefits humanity...' Within this transformation we may recognize the influence of the spirit of our age, Michael.

The inspiration of Elijah Muhammad

Following Malcolm X's murder Elijah Muhammad com-mented: 'We didn't want to kill Malcolm! His foolish teaching would bring him to his own end! I am not going to let the crackpots destroy the good things Allah sent to you and me!'[37] Indeed, Malcolm X's awakening recognition of the individual human being was a threat to the views Elijah Muhammad represented. In his central work, *Message to the Black Man in America*, Elijah Muhammad's teachings are clearly articulated: the 'whole Caucasian [white] race is a race of devils'.[38] On the other hand, 'Allah has decided to place us [the black race] on the top... We are the mighty, the wise, the best . . .'[39] He continues: 'Surely, if the Father of the two peoples, black and white, were the same, the two would love each other because they are of the same flesh and blood. It is natural then for them to love each other. Again, it is not unnatural then for a member or members of a different race or nation not to love the non-member of their race or nation as their own.'[40] Integration is '. . . opposed by God, Himself. It is time that the two people should separate.'

According to Elijah Muhammad, God made the black race, whereas the white race was created by an evil scientist named Yakub. Sixty-six trillion years ago a great explosion caused the Earth to separate from the Moon. This was brought about by God who, frustrated by the fact that the people on Earth did not speak one language, packed the centre of the Earth with dynamite and 'decided to kill us by destroying our planet'.[41] He failed, however, and the black tribe of Shabazz continued to live on Earth in Egypt and Arabia. The creation of the white race, however, occurred relatively recently. Some 6,600 years ago a man named Yakub, a member of the black race, was born in Mecca.[42] Through discovering the science of genetics, Yakub learned that he could create a white race which would rule the black people. At the age of 18 he began preaching on the streets and gathering adherents by promising people that he would make others work for them. The authorities in Mecca began to be concerned by this teaching and started arresting his followers, but the numbers of Yakub's people continued to grow. Eventually the jails were full of Yakub's devotees and Yakub himself was arrested, but his popularity still increased. And so finally the king struck a bargain with Yakub, who agreed to take his 59,999-strong entourage to live on the island of Patmos in the Aegean in return for 20 years funding of his new community.

Through controlling marriages and procreation, and a secret genocidal policy towards black babies, Yakub ensured that after 200 years only brown babies were born on the island. After another 200 years only yellow or red babies were born; and finally, after another 200 years, Mr Yakub 'had an all-pale white race of people' on the island. Yakub had died after 150 years, but had left instructions to his people which they observed. 'When you become unalike (white), you may return to the Holy Land and people, from which you were exiled,' he told them. This 'devil' race was pale white with blue eyes, and called Caucasian (which, according to Elijah Muhammad, means 'one whose evil effect is not confined to oneself alone, but affects others').

The devil white race then returned to live among the black people, where they created strife and disturbance. The king realized the problem and instructed his folk to drive the devil white race out from 'Paradise', across the Arabian desert, to Europe. There they were exiled for 2,000 years and became savages living in caves. After this period, Allah sent Moses to recivilize the white race. However, this was a difficult task as this race was so barbaric. Elijah Muhammad describes one incident when Moses became so upset with the white race that he tricked 300 of its members to stand on a mountainside where he had hidden 'a few sticks of dynamite' and, lighting the fuse, killed them all. When the Imans complained to Moses about the immoral nature of this episode, Moses protested: 'If you only knew how much trouble these devils give me, you would do as I do.'

Eventually, as had been prophesied, the devil white race gained control of 'Original Man' (the black race) and subjected him until the present time. Elijah Muhammad explains that the white race is called 'mankind' because 'they are in the image and likeness of a human being (black man)'. However, their pale skin and blue eyes prove that 'there can't be any sincere love and friendship for them'. For the black people have 'a heart of gold, love and mercy', but the whites do not. Instead, they are characterized by treachery, evil and wrong-doing.

To round off this potent teaching, Elijah Muhammad gives a picture of the coming Judgment and Apocalypse during which the white devil race will be destroyed and the black race will remain on Earth in a physical paradise. This destruction of the 'present world of the enemies of Allah' (the white race) will be carried out by a giant 'wheel-shaped plane', known as 'the Mother of Planets', which carries 'fifteen hundred bombing planes with the most deadliest explosives'.[43] After the annihilation of the white devil race and his world, the Earth will become a 'Heaven of the righteous forever', with no 'sickness, no hospitals, no insane asylums, no gambling, no cursing, or swearing ... fear, grief or sorrow.' The black race on Earth 'will be clothed in silk interwoven with gold and eat the best of food'.[44]

From one perspective it is apparent that Elijah Muhammad's understanding of race is an extreme reaction to contrary theories of (white) racial superiority. But while racist doctrines are not altogether uncommon, Elijah Muhammad's theological justification is somewhat unusual and portentous. However, it is principally the vehement materialism of his teaching, which provides the foundation for this 'theology', that is most remarkable; for together with the descent into base matter of the concepts of 'God' and 'Devil', 'Heaven' and 'Hell', the spirit is relegated to an insignificant status. Thus, 'God is a man and we just cannot make Him other than man, lest we make Him an inferior one; for man's intelligence has no equal in other than man. His wisdom is infinite; capable of accomplishing anything that His brain can conceive. A spirit is subjected to us and not we to the spirit.'[45] He urges us therefore to see the coming of the 'Son of Man' as a physical man '... and not the coming of a "spirit". Let that one among you who believes God is other than man prove it!' At another point, referring to the Last Judgment, he asks: 'How can a spirit be our judge when we cannot see a spirit?'

This materialistic revelation is presented as a glorious gift to the black peoples of the Earth. 'The belief in a God other than man (a spirit) Allah has taught me goes back into the millions of years ... because the knowledge of God was kept as a secret from the public. This is the first time that it has ever been revealed, and we, the poor rejected and despised people, are blessed to be the first of all the people of Earth to receive this secret knowledge of God.'[46] An integral part of this teaching is a rejection of Christ as a divine Being. As with the instruction of the Koran and traditional Islam, Jesus is respected as a prophet, but the idea of any spiritual entity connected with Jesus or Christ is dismissed by Elijah Muhammad. Thus, his followers '...must get away from the old slavery teaching that Jesus, who was killed 2,000 years ago, is still alive somewhere waiting and listening to their prayers.'[47] Moreover, 'Christianity was [merely] a religion organized and backed by the devils for the purpose of making slaves of black mankind.'[48, 49]

Just as it is probable that Nazi ideology had occult roots,[50] so it is not inconceivable that the doctrine of the Nation of Islam is inspired from a hidden source. A clue to this question may be found in remarks made by Rudolf Steiner regarding the karmic consequences of western Europe's 'countless acts of injustice' in the East 'against the bearers of an old spiritual culture and its occult secrets'.[51] As one consequence of this, '... India, which had suffered from the suppression of its own occultism, took the first opportunity for karmic revenge' by infecting occultism in the West 'with its own form of egotistic national occultism' (to be found, for example, in H. P. Blavatsky's *The Secret Doctrine*). 'Today the Tibetan, Indian and even the Egyptian initiations all have only a partial human interest at heart; they want only to take revenge on the West for the suppression of eastern occultism, and for the conquest of the East by the materialistic resources of the western world.'[52, 53]

In one of H. B. Blavatsky's lesser known works, a travel

diary published as *From the Caves and Jungles of Hindustan*, she speaks of an eastern mahatma named Gulab-Lal-Singh who accompanies her party on its travels. This master— whom her colleague Colonel Olcott referred to as 'a real Adept ... with whom I have had to do'[54]—is described by Blavatsky as belonging '... to the sect of raja-yogins, initiated into the mysteries of magic, alchemy, and various other occult sciences of India.'[55] At one point in the narrative she reports that Gulab-Lal-Singh 'hates and despises' the white race.[56] As Sergei O. Prokofieff points out, these words 'fully correspond in their emotional mood to Rudolf Steiner's remarks ... about the efforts of Tibeto-Indian initiates to take vengeance upon the western world on behalf of suppressed eastern occultism'.[57]

We could conclude from the above that Gulab-Lal-Singh might well represent an actual example of an eastern initiate of the type that Rudolf Steiner refers to. Could W. D. Fard similarly have been a genuine master from the East? Like Gulab-Lal-Singh, W. D. Fard's pupil Elijah Muhammad seemed to 'hate and despise' the entire white race, and within his invectives against Christianity, his picture of Jesus Christ as one prophet among many others, and his materialization of spiritual concepts,[58] we can recognize parallels to the distorted occultism that Rudolf Steiner speaks of.

The question of whether 'the Master' W. D. Fard was an eastern occultist cannot, of course, be substantiated without detailed research. Nevertheless, from the information available certain clues would suggest that such a possibility is not altogether unlikely. In his biography of Malcolm X, George Perry points out that Fard—who Elijah Muhammad claimed was 'God in person'—'looked white', but said he was a 'light-skinned Negro' and 'a brother from the East'.[59] Elijah Muhammad adds that Fard 'had to have a body that would be part of each side (black and white), half and half' so that 'he is able to go among both black and white without being discovered or recognized'.[60] In 1934 Fard apparently 'disappeared'. Elijah Muhammad states that he 'chose to suffer three and a half years' in America, after which he returned to Mecca.

In his important work *The Masters Revealed*,[61] K. Paul Johnson attempts to identify the 'adepts' and 'mahatmas' of H. P. Blavatsky as actual historical personalities. Johnson associates Blavatsky's mahatma Gulab-Lal-Singh with the Maharaja Ranbir Singh of Kashmir. Whether similar research could prove that 'the Master' W. D. Fard was truly a historical personage from the East remains to be seen. Certainly, his possible identity as an initiate with only 'a partial human interest at heart' (as Rudolf Steiner describes the present Tibetan, Indian and Egyptian initiations) would provide a good explanation for his racially-orientated philosophy. Suffice to say, however, in carrying out his mission and helping to establish the Nation of Islam and its teachings, he (or, at least, Elijah Muhammad) helped fulfil the egoistic wishes of the occult brotherhoods that seek 'to take revenge on the West'.[62]

THE QUESTION OF RACE, II

A Spiritual Perspective

In the previous chapter, in reflecting on the Nation of Islam and events such as the beating of Rodney King and the subsequent riots in the USA, we have seen hostilities that arise primarily out of a consciousness of the human being's physical inheritance. We must now ask what an anthroposophical approach can contribute to the difficult and emotive subject of race. Rudolf Steiner was adamant that anthroposophy had a role to play in bringing healing to the social and political spheres. In 1917, in the midst of the First World War, he proclaimed: '...No matter how much one believes that the concepts customary outside spiritual science today will enable us to emerge out of the chaos, it will not happen; for within the reality the spirit prevails... In the future politics and social science will need something for which only spiritual science can provide the foundation.'[1]

In attempting to throw light on the question of race, we will focus on the results of Rudolf Steiner's spiritual-scientific research. While Steiner spoke on this subject from many and varied perspectives, our concerns here are (a) to study race in the context of an anthroposophical picture of human evolution, and (b) to consider the factor of physical inheritance within the manifold influences which work on the modern human being.

Race in the context of human evolution

If we wish to discover the origins of race in human evolution, we must travel back in time to the Atlantean period of the incarnation of the Earth.[2] It was here that the original formation of the races took place through a complex process involving the co-operation of various spiritual beings, particularly the Spirits of Form (also called the Elohim) and the 'backward' or 'abnormal' Spirits of Form, and the influence of reflected planetary forces.[3] In the lecture course published as *The Mission of the Individual Folk Souls* Steiner describes how the Elohim—divided into six working from the Sun and the seventh, Yahveh, from the Moon—rayed down forces onto the Earth. If only those Elohim working from the Sun had been active in a particular region of the Earth's surface, then a single human race would have developed that was, from the beginning, based on the 'I' principle, i.e. that which is universally human. However, through the intervention of the abnormal Spirits of Form working from various planets—for example Mercury and Jupiter—several individual races were created through a modification of the universally human forces of the Elohim.

The forces of the abnormal Spirits of Form streaming down upon the Earth from the various planets were arrested by the Earth and then rayed outward again from its centre to a particular geographical region, thus creating the various primal races.[4] The influences of the forces of the backward Spirits of Form were initially associated only with a particular geographical region, but later came to be passed on through inheritance ('... racial characteristics were hereditary from the beginning of the Atlantean epoch up to our post-Atlantean epoch').[5]

However, when considering the concept of race through the perspective of evolution as given in Anthroposophy, we should recognize that the original idea of 'race'—in the Atlantean period as described above—is no longer directly relevant to our present stage of evolution. In the present post-Atlantean epoch it is not even appropriate to speak of races, for:

... we speak of ages of civilization, in contradistinction to races. All that is connected with the idea of race is still the remains of the epoch preceding our own, namely, the Atlantean. We are now living in the age of cultural epochs. Atlantis was the age in which seven great races developed ... Of course the fruits of this race development extend into our epoch, and for this reason races are still spoken of today, but they are really mixtures and are quite unlike those distinct races of the Atlantean epoch. Today the idea of civilization has already superseded the idea of race.[6]

This proper designation of the word 'race' to the Atlantean epoch is affirmed in the series of lectures published as *Universe Earth and Man*:

While it is true that the races have arisen through this [Atlantean epoch], it is incorrect to speak of races in the far back Lemurian epoch; and in our own epoch the idea of race will gradually disappear along with all the differences that are a relic of earlier times. We speak of races, but all that remains of these today are relics of differences that existed in Atlantean times, and the idea of race has now lost its original meaning.[7]

The point is amplified in another lecture delivered in 1908. Here Steiner explains that the principle of evolution '... is from the group-soul nature to the individual soul'.[8] During Atlantean times, the human being experienced a vivid consciousness of his group soul. The advance '... from group soul to individual soul has taken place in times lying very near our own ... If we look at groups instead of souls, we have family connections, connections of tribe and nation, and finally connected races. The race corresponds to a group soul. All these group connections of early humanity are what man outgrows and the more we advance the more the race conception loses its meaning.'[9]

The old group relationships worked directly through the blood. 'There [in ancient times] we find that what is related by blood loves its own; it loves because love is implanted by the laws of nature; and the further we go the more we find that all those consider themselves as belonging to one another and loving one another who have had love implanted by the laws of nature, by the forces appertaining to the external form.'[10] However, free evolutionary development can only be undertaken

> ... through human beings being severed from the group-soul quality; through one human being confronting another; only thus can true love develop. Where egos are united within the group-soul there is no true love. Beings must be separated from each other so that love may be offered as a free gift... This is why an increasing individualism and a uniting of separate individuals had to come about on Earth ... thus man continued gradually to mature that he might eventually receive the highest potency of love—the Christ principle, which expressed its nature in the words, 'He who does not forsake father, mother, son, and daughter, he who does not take up his cross and follow Me, is not worthy of Me.' These words are not to be understood trivially, but in the sense that, through reception of the Christ principle, the ancient blood-brotherhood had to assume a new form, a feeling of 'belonging to each other' which, regardless of material foundations, must pass from soul to soul, from person to person.[11]

From the above quotations we are given a clear conception of the stream of evolution as it leads from the old group consciousness to a modern individual consciousness. This individual consciousness is a direct result of the gradual incarnation of the 'I' or ego within the human being. The individual 'I' is in turn directly connected to the Christ principle[12]—the higher self—which, as a 'spark of the

divine', acts as a developing power, allowing for a transformation and redemption of the lower nature.

In a lecture entitled 'The Spiritual Unity of Mankind
through the Christ-impulse' Steiner accentuates the significance of Christ in relation to race, evolution and the
development of the 'I' or ego. The original intention of the
divine powers was that the different races would appear as
a succession. This plan would have led to a harmonious
type of humanity in our present time. By the fourth post-
Atlantean period, however, a crisis had arisen: there existed
a real danger that seven groups of human beings could
have developed, as different as the several groups of animals. 'The one name "Man" for all human beings on Earth
would have seemed wrong; we should have had seven
designations for seven different groups of beings on Earth,
and not a single designation for humanity spread over all
the Earth.'[13]

This potential disaster was averted, however, by the
Mystery of Golgotha. Through the incarnation of Christ, the
possibility emerged for a unification of all humanity.
However, Steiner emphasizes the good possibilities that
arose from the physical splitting of races by the adversary
forces.

> First the gods allowed man to be 'split up' as the result of
> opposing forces, in order that later, after the bodily nature
> had been thus split up, he could in his spiritual nature,
> through Christ, again be brought into a unity ... *Externally*
> human beings are becoming more and more different; the
> result will be that there is no uniformity, but diversity over
> the Earth, and that people must exert all the more force
> from *within* outwards in order to attain unity.[14]

There will inevitably be setbacks, he warns, but a spiritual
unity of humanity over the whole Earth can be attained
through Christ (but not necessarily in the form of outward
Christianity) and free human effort.

In the future, little will depend upon whether what *is* the Christ is also *called* by the Name of Christ; but very much will depend upon the fact that in the Christ people seek spiritually the Uniter of the whole of humanity, and that they accept the idea that external diversity will become greater and greater in the world... Human beings must face calmly and courageously the diversity and multiplicity of human nature, because they know that a Word can be brought into all human diversities that is not merely a word of speech but a word of power... Into whatever group of human beings we bear our Ego, we may also bear the power that comes from the Word 'Not I, but the Christ in me'. With this we bear into the group something that does not belong to a single group but to the whole of humanity, and it is this alone that can lead to a true spiritual understanding of Christianity.[15]

Such a unity—of individual egos united by Christ—can already be nurtured in groups such as the Anthroposophical Society, where in freedom spiritual knowledge can be a binding force: 'The attempt had to be made to create a group in which people find themselves together without the differentiation of the ancient group soul's nature, and there will be many such associations in the future. Then we shall no longer have to speak of racial connections but of intellectual-ethical-moral aspects with regard to the associations that are formed.'[16] Such free associations allow different spiritual beings to work as 'group souls', but in such a way that is compatible with the human being's complete freedom and individuality. 'The more that associations are formed where feelings of fellowship are developed with complete freedom, the more lofty beings will descend and the more rapidly the earthly planet will be spiritualized.'[17]

In the future we may expect a completely different, non-racial, organization of humanity.

Humanity will be differentiated in the future even more than in the past; it will be divided into categories, but not in an arbitrary way; from their own spiritual inner capacities individuals will come to know that they must work together for the whole social body ... They will say: One must do this, the other must do that. Division of work even to the smallest detail will take place; work will be so organized that a holder of this or that position will not find it necessary to impose his authority on others ... Humanity will be divided [in the seventh post-Atlantean epoch] according to differences in intellect and morals ...[18]

Thus we see the evolutionary development from the group-soul nature connected by the blood, through a process of individualization, and finally a return to a truly spiritual community. This development is brought about by the deed of Christ, and the individual striving of free human beings.

Physical inheritance and the modern human being

From the point of view of spiritual science, the human being is formed and developed under the influence of manifold spiritual and physical forces. To take a single factor—such as that of physical inheritance—and make it an all-important principle is thus to ignore many other influences on the nature and character of the modern human being. To attain a full picture of the modern human being it is necessary to study some of these numerous shaping powers. A comprehensive picture cannot be given within this short essay; however, an attempt will be made briefly to indicate some of the factors which need to be considered if a true wisdom of man—Anthroposophy—is to be striven for.

(i) Forces which rise from the Earth

Of the many powers which work on the modern human being independently of his physical nature are the forces that rise from the Earth. 'In accordance with geographical differentiations, the most varied forces stream up out of the various territories.'[19] These forces—which are '...geographic; they are not ethnographic, not national, but purely geographic forces'[20]—can have an effect, for example, on the human 'double'. In the region of Russia they help to overcome the nature of the double, while parts of America allow a kinship to develop with the 'Mephistophelian-ahrimanic nature'.

When speaking of this subject in 1917, in relation to the terrestrial forces which emanate from the Earth in Ireland, Rudolf Steiner warned that one should not 'confuse what really develops within the human being with the characteristics of the earthly organism in a definite territory'. However, from knowledge of such forces '...should emerge a factor, among many factors...One must gather everything together, to be created into a science of the forming of human conditions on Earth. Until this comes about no true healing can come into the arrangement of public affairs.'[21]

(ii) The physical nature

In 'gathering everything together' to create a science of the human conditions on Earth it would be incorrect to eradicate completely the factor of physical heredity. Our present races—as remnants of the Atlantean period—may be 'mixtures' and 'relics', but it would be wrong to state that the hereditary principle is non-existent. One example of how the physical nature can affect the inner human being will be given. In a lecture on the occult significance of the blood in relation to modern intellectual consciousness, Rudolf Steiner relates humanity's ancient, dreamy, clairvoyance to the principle of endogamy (the custom of marrying only within clan or tribe).[22] Our present consciousness is owed to the introduction of exogamy: '...in an unmixed blood is expressed the power of the ancestral life, and in a mixed blood the power of personal experience.'[23]

While such spiritual-scientific knowledge has a relevance, Steiner emphasizes that a philosophy based solely on the hereditary principle would imprison the human being in materialism.

> The first thing people ask about a child nowadays is from whom it has got this or that characteristic. And the reply, however, is seldom that the child has it as a result of this or that particular experience in the spiritual world. People look instead to see whether it comes from the grandmother or grandfather, and so on. The more this emerges in individual people—not merely as a theory but as a feeling, a feeling of dependence on purely earthly inherited characteristics—the more oppressive and dreadful will it gradually become... This will arise more and more: that the human being will feel his existence to be worthless if he cannot feel it to be anything other than the sum total of what has been implanted in his blood and in his other organs by physically inherited characteristics.[24]

In the lecture course published as *The Karma of Untruthfulness*, a suggestion is given as to what a more spiritual picture can lead to.

> Someone who does not study spiritual science can only say: I am connected to my nationality through my blood, through my blood I defend what lives in my nation, it is my blood that obliges me to identify with my nationality. One who does study spiritual science, however, must answer: I am connected with my nationality through my karma, for this is a part of my karma. As soon as concepts of karma are brought into the question, the whole relationship becomes much more spiritual.[25]

The point is elucidated further in an earlier lecture where Steiner speaks of the human soul's need for '... a certain degree of intensity in its impulses'. 'If it cannot reach up to ideas, it will take this intensity from elsewhere, from obscure, unconscious soul forces, from forces that rush up from the spirit of the blood.'[26]

(iii) Nation and the Folk Soul

We are led by the above to the significant influence of nation. However, it is important at this point to distinguish clearly between the concepts of 'race' and 'nation', and to understand their proper roles in evolution. In Rudolf Steiner's words: 'A nation is not a race. The concept of nation has nothing to do with that of race.'[27] 'The evolution of races is interrupted to make way for the evolution of nations, i.e. nations develop out of races ... The nation occupies an intermediate position between the race and the individual.'[28] Further on in the same lecture he says: '... in our own time the national characteristics prepare in their turn the breakdown of the racial characteristics and begin to eradicate them.'

From an anthroposophical grounding, we may recognize the legitimate role of nations today—each led and nurtured by an archangelic being, or Folk Soul—and their individual destinies. (Their tasks are elaborated in many of Rudolf Steiner's lectures.) The Folk Soul helps provide a national 'character'. However, a nation can embrace peoples who speak different languages—for example Switzerland—for the forces that come from the individual Folk Souls do not work on the basis of race, but through the etheric body. Steiner clarifies this in the following words: 'We can easily picture therefore a people inhabiting a certain territory; over this people extends the etheric aura of the people into which the forces of the Folk Spirit work, modifying the etheric body of the human being.' In the same lecture Steiner indicates the significance of the human being's karmic connection with the Folk Soul: 'The Angels impel him towards the locality ordained for him, so that the feelings of the people should concur in the great ordinances of the Archangels.'[29]

As with the dangers attached to viewing physical inheritance as an all-important principle, so the idea of 'nation' also has its shadow-side.

> The great crisis of the second decade of the twentieth century was ushered in when those who were supposed to be leading the nations ... began talking about organizing mankind according to the will of its individual nations. It was indeed in our recent times that national chauvinism was aroused in its very worst sense. And it is national chauvinism that is ringing through the whole civilized world today. This is merely the social counterpoint of the utterly reactionary world-view that tries to trace everything back to inherited characteristics... Nothing, perhaps, shows more clearly the materialism of modern times, its denial of everything spiritual, than the emergence of the principle of nationalism.[30]

In 1917 Steiner reiterated this point, indicating materialistic thinking as the cause of the symptom:

> ...it is not ideas which strive towards harmonious co-existence of human beings on Earth—in other words, not Christian ideas—which are uppermost, but those which, in utmost excess, divide mankind and lead back to cultural periods which one might suppose to have been long overcome. The monstrous anomaly lies in the way nationalism was so forcefully able to take hold of the nations as they lived side by side in the nineteenth century. This shows that in their soul development human beings have not kept pace with material progress.[31]

(iv) The influence of the Time Spirit

Another important spiritual force which works on all human beings today, independent of nation or race, is that which comes from the present Time Spirit. For, '. . . in every age there is something that transcends the Folk Soul, which can bring the various Folk Souls together, something that is more or less universally understood. This is the *Zeitgeist* or Time Spirit.'[32] As related in the story of Malcolm X, the tendency of the present Time Spirit, Michael, is to fight the 'spirits of falsehood' which seek to create tension between the races. The impulse deriving from the spiritual worlds, under the regency of Michael, is to 'pour a cosmopolitan element over mankind'.[33]

(v) The ego or 'I'

In our considerations of the many forces working on the consciousness of the modern human being, perhaps the most important factor is that of the individual ego or 'I'. This spiritual aspect of each human being is—as we have seen in our survey of the evolution of consciousness—the element which has created the human being's increasing individualization from the previous racial and other types of group-soul consciousness. It is this 'I' which allows for the transformation of the lower bodies (the physical, etheric and astral bodies) into the higher, refined spiritual bodies (Spirit Self, Life Spirit and Spirit Man)—giving the possibility for growth and development.

The 'I' carries the essence of our being—our personal 'individuality'—from incarnation to incarnation. In this respect it is important to note that this individual nature incarnates over time into the physical bodies of different races and nations, experiencing the fruits of different peoples and cultures.

(vi) The Christ Being

The 'I', as shown earlier, is integrally connected to the Christ Being. A new individual experience of Christ, who brings about the transformative power in Earth evolution, can ultimately lead to the healing of social divisions between peoples—tribes, nations, or races. ('The solutions to our social problems will be found to the degree in which human beings are able to feel the Christ-impulse in their souls.')[34] A knowledge of the spiritual nature of the world and humanity is a firm grounding for a realization of this Christ-impulse in the souls of human beings. Thus, man should recognize that he is a

> ...cosmic being, a being belonging to the whole universe. On the one side the human being will feel himself bound to the Earth; on the other he will feel himself to be a cosmic being ... And when this is no longer mere theory but is experienced by individual human beings whose karma enables them to grow beyond the trivial feelings of today—when humanity comes to feel disgust at the thought of purely inherited characteristics and at the emotions engendered by chauvinism and turns against all this—only then will a kind of reverse begin. The human being will feel himself to be a cosmic being.[35]

This knowledge that the human being is a cosmic being is to be found in the modern spiritual science of Anthroposophy. Through this modern wisdom of the human being we see that, as a *cosmic* being, man lives under the sway of manifold spiritual influences, extending beyond those of geographic location, physical organism and Folk Soul. And this spiritual path of Anthroposophy is not restricted to country, nation or race. As Ita Wegman, one of its early pioneers, asserts: 'Anthroposophy must become even more than hitherto cosmopolitan, must not be bottled up by groups of people nor remain limited to special countries. It is for everyone throughout the whole world. That is Michael's will. He will have love for the world spread over all mankind.'[36] And as Rudolf Steiner affirms: '...a spiritual-scientific world view is intent upon creating something that can really be accepted by all nations in all regions. For people must advance in the mutual exchange of their spiritual treasures.'[37]

As we may witness from the following quotation, Rudolf Steiner was adamant that true Anthroposophy could not be a sectarian philosophy, and indeed that it contained the seeds for universal social renewal: 'We can best serve mankind if we develop our particular talents so as to offer them to the whole of humanity as a sacrifice which we bring to the progressive development of culture', for '...what alone accords with anthroposophical teaching is that we should unselfishly dedicate the best that is in us, our sympathy and compassion, to the well-being of all mankind... Spiritual science, as we shall realize more and more clearly, will bring an end to the divisions of mankind.'[38]

APPENDIX:
READING THE SIGNS OF THE TIMES

Anthroposophy and Contemporary Culture

An 'interpretation of reality'

As we approach the close of the twentieth century, our media-dominated lives are saturated to an unprecedented degree with countless images, pictures, messages, and abundant 'information'. From a spiritual perspective it could be said that much of what comes towards us in this way—through mediums such as advertising, television, radio, newspapers and computer technology—represents a particular version or reading of 'reality'. Although many people are unaware or unconscious that such an *interpretation* of reality is continually taking place, this is nevertheless the case. The philosophy that is the basis for this interpretation is called 'materialism'—an understanding of the world that excludes, by definition, anything of a soul or spiritual nature, or reduces such phenomena to materialistic paradigms (for example, the notion that human thought is merely the result of biological processes in the brain). As suggested, this world-view of materialism determines much of the understanding and the underlying assumptions of modern life.

Although in the West our entire culture is permeated by this philosophy of materialism, nevertheless its dissemination is relatively subtle. After all, we live in a society that is largely 'free'—where there is little outward political repression of spiritual or religious life. In comparison, during the 72 years of Communist rule in Soviet Russia materialism was venerated officially as a science, and spirituality and religion—'the opiate of the masses'—were carefully restricted. Many of the Communist regimes in the East adhered to what Marx and Engels referred to as 'scientific materialism', an atheistic philosophy which purports to prove that the spirit does not, and cannot, exist. However, since it cannot actually be proved scientifically that the spirit does not exist, a true appraisal of scientific materialism would conclude that it is in nature far closer to a religion than a science. Ironically, the atheist in effect 'believes' or has faith in the notion that the spirit does not exist. Such a belief is, in turn, as 'naive' as that of the simple person who has faith in the existence of God or the spirit.

The science of the spirit

In contrast to the naive and unscientific nature of atheism or scientific materialism, Rudolf Steiner set out to found a truly *scientific* approach to comprehending the world, which does not rely on religious faith or belief. Thus, as with all genuine sciences, he laid down a methodology (to be found in his most fundamental works)[1] to demonstrate how one could repeat the results of his clairvoyant spiritual-scientific research. However, unlike other sciences, the science of the spirit (Anthroposophy) requires the researcher to develop new faculties that will enable him or her to perceive realms of existence hidden to the physical eye. Such faculties are necessary if one is to prove or disprove the results of Rudolf Steiner's clairvoyant research.[2] The serious student can begin on this path by following the methods of spiritual development outlined in Rudolf Steiner's books, for example his meditation manual *Knowledge of the Higher Worlds*.[3] Given the necessary commitment and perseverance, the spiritual student will be able to develop new esoteric ways of knowing, and the basic results of Rudolf Steiner's own experimentation and research into spiritual, non-sensory realities will become evident to him or her.

Unlike the old Mystery schools, where one had to be accepted into an exclusive group by undergoing various intricate initiation ceremonies, this path is open to any serious enquirer today. However, while it is perfectly possible to develop higher spiritual capabilities through the above means, such a goal may require a lifetime of devoted work. With regard to the great initiates of history, their particular gifts are often the fruits of many incarnations of intense preparation. Thus it is not surprising that in the case of the twentieth-century initiate Rudolf Steiner we may—in studying the detailed results of his clairvoyant research in many fields (published in literally hundreds of volumes in the original German)—feel quite overawed by the depth and profundity of his knowledge. We should be aware of the special destiny and abilities with which such an individual descends to earth.

Developing clear judgement

Of course, the above realization should not stop us from working diligently to develop spiritual faculties, and furthermore to understand the need today for an increasing number of individuals who *know* the reality of the spiritual dimension from direct experience. Nevertheless, regardless of where we are in our personal development of clairvoyance, there is a basic faculty which we can all begin to train immediately, and which can have a tremendously positive effect on the world. This human quality (which is also one of the basic requirements on the path of initiation) is, in Rudolf Steiner's words, 'an unconditionally sound, reliable power of judgement' which enables the individual 'to distinguish true reality from illusion...'[4] Such an ability is of course absolutely necessary when one is beginning to have spiritual experiences, but it is also important to develop such a judgement, based on clear unprejudiced thinking, in everyday life. If such a striving for truth—a desire to allow what is 'real' to reveal itself to us—is nurtured, then we begin to permeate our entire being with the attitude of modern spiritual science.

In developing such a faculty of lucid thinking, the spiritual student will do well also to bear in mind three qualities of soul which, as Rudolf Steiner warned members of the Anthroposophical Society, are 'three great enemies'.[5] These are naivety, illusion and a lack of discrimination. If such qualities are countered, and a faculty of sound judgement is developed, then the individual is truly on the modern spiritual path—a way of development that bears little resemblance to the popular image of the 'spiritual' person, obsessed with the religious or occult, who has lost touch with everyday reality.

The individual on the modern spiritual path will also be aided by an earnest study of the results of true spiritual research ('the study of spiritual science'). Such a penetration into a new world of concepts that are unavailable through everyday perception will enable the student to expand his or her consciousness to encompass as yet unknown realms of knowledge. By gaining such new conceptions (a living Anthroposophy) and applying these to contemporary life and culture, the individual can begin to delve beneath the outer semblance of reality, through to the deeper occult forces which underlie human evolution.

Approaching contemporary culture

With the above in mind, let us return to the question of the proper response to, and comprehension of, contemporary popular culture. When confronted with the sensory assault of various modern mediums such as television, we are simultaneously challenged with the question of how we should respond to the deluge of information and images with which they present us. While many people find themselves seduced, comforted and absorbed by popular culture, others—particularly those seeking a 'spiritual' existence—are so overwhelmed that they seek refuge by avoiding all its manifestations (i.e. by not buying newspapers or watching television, protecting themselves from film, popular music, and so on). The dangers of the former path are self-evident: a thorough self-identification with the materialistic culture of our time can lead to a hardening and creeping insensitivity towards anything spiritual. In terms of Rudolf Steiner's cosmic picture of the dual nature of evil, one would be adhering strongly to the path of Ahriman, which leads to an eventual rejection of the spirit. However, the other way—avoiding all forms of contemporary culture—is just as dangerous. Here one is leaning towards the other extreme, the path of Lucifer, where rejection of material reality leads to the creation of an illusory 'spiritual' fantasy. On this path the individual loses the inclination to tackle the challenges of everyday life, increasingly seeking spiritual ecstasy. (Such a path culminates in a desire to escape from the cycle of birth and death—the goal of many forms of eastern teaching to be found in the West today.)

However, through following the modern spiritual path most suited to western consciousness, Anthroposophy, we can discover a third, middle, way to cope with contemporary culture. Taking this approach we stimulate a great interest in modern life and the world around us. But, by awakening the faculties of clear thought and discrimination mentioned earlier, we seek to *understand* what we experience with a scientific attitude that does not, however, exclude the soul and spirit. Through such striving we are provided with the means potentially to cognize the non-physical forces at work all around, while simultaneously becoming aware of the false 'realities' of materialism which are promoted with such vigour by our society today. We can thus live within the existing world as truly modern individuals—enjoying the fruits of contemporary life—without compromising our metaphysical striving.

The challenge of modern media

And yet there is no doubt that this is a difficult and somewhat dangerous path; for the more sophisticated and all-embracing certain types of media become the more difficult it is to perceive the realities of the physical world, let alone occult forces at work behind physical events. A powerful example of this danger is provided by the popular perception of the Gulf War of 1991. As journalist Maggie O'Kane, who has made an extensive study of the background to the war,[6] writes: 'Somehow during the Gulf War, the presence of so many reporters and TV crews gave the public at home the impression that they were seeing and learning more than their parents and grandparents had ... in earlier wars. They weren't.'[7] This most televised war in history, with 24-hour coverage on the cable channel CNN, was presented as a bloodless, giant video game in which laser-guided missiles hit their targets with deadly accuracy. The truth, which was quite different, was carefully concealed by the western governments who expertly manipulated the news media. Thus the full horror of the 1–2,000 Iraqi soldiers buried alive in trenches by US bulldozers, the 489 napalm bombs dropped by US Marines on trenches, the blanket bombing by B52 bombers which killed more than 30,000 soldiers, and the many thousands of retreating conscripts killed on the 'turkey shoot' of the Basra road, were kept off the television screen.

Another rather insidious example shows how powerful the media was in manipulating public perceptions of the war. In November 1990 the Kuwaiti government was provided with a key news story by the public relations firm Hill & Knowlton, which they had hired for millions of dollars. In the first days of the invasion, it was reported, Iraqi troops had gone into a Kuwaiti hospital where they tore sick babies from incubators and left them to die on the cold floor. The story had a major effect on the direction of the war (George Bush referred to it in five speeches) but, as Maggie O'Kane shows, it was a complete fabrication.

The intention in referring to the above examples is not to make partisan political points; many terrible things could also be written about the Iraqi conduct before and during the war (such as their extensive use of chemical weapons or their brutal treatment of ethnic groups).[8] It could further be objected that what is described above is not extraordinary in war, and that propaganda and misinformation have been used by all sides throughout history. While there is some truth to such a contention, it is nevertheless a fact that today the scale of deception possible through the media, and demonstrated during the Gulf War, is unprecedented. Thus our example seeks to prove that, as stated earlier, the task of comprehending the physical reality of life—let alone the spiritual reality— becomes ever more complicated.

It could likewise be said of other modern mediums that it becomes increasingly difficult to tell illusion from reality. Special effects in film are often dazzlingly convincing; the crystal-clear sound quality of digital recordings emulates live music; and the increasing sophistication of 'virtual reality' computer games draws us into their fake world. Everywhere, the false realities of materialism gain strength. Such a situation, however, makes it all the more urgent for spiritually-minded individuals to tread the 'third way' described above, taking an interest in all manifestations of contemporary culture and striving to *understand* them. Such a response can then begin to have a positive effect on the world, as will be explained below.

From symptom to reality

An important key to a spiritual understanding of life is to overcome the illusion that events and phenomena on the physical plane are the results of purely material causes or factors. A materialistic approach to history, for example, assumes that history is determined by outward events— effects created by material causes. In contrast, Rudolf Steiner's approach to history, as revealed in his many studies of contemporary events,[9] treats outer events only as symptoms. One must learn to read such symptoms and see how they point to the full occult reality behind the material causes. An outstanding example of a study of modern history using this method is found in Sergei O. Prokofieff's book *The Spiritual Origins of Eastern Europe and the Future Mysteries of the Holy Grail.*[10] In this work Prokofieff undertakes a 'symptomatological' approach to Russian history, exemplified in his consideration of twentieth-century history, which focuses on four levels of reality: the outer, purely earthly events, the 'occult-historical' level, and two further 'metahistorical' and spiritual dimensions. As he states:

> Only against the background of such a historical and metahistorical panorama, imbued as it is with a concrete knowledge of the aims and intentions of the good and evil forces which will ever and again continue to struggle for their right to guide eastern Europe and to a certain extent the whole of humanity, can the individual facts and phenomena be revealed in accordance with their true nature.
>
> ...For in themselves, divorced from the great perspectives of the spiritual-historical evolution of mankind, these events—and also over-hasty judgements of them— may easily prove to be 'maya', illusion, the expression of unconscious wishes whose consequences would, however, be disastrous for the whole of human evolution.

And if in the wider world, to the extent that it lies far removed from a spiritual-scientific view of historical processes, it is in practice virtually impossible to avoid such illusory judgements, so it is all the more necessary to strive on the foundation of Anthroposophy with all one's forces towards judgements which correspond to the *full* reality; that is, not only with regard to outward history but also to the spiritual dimension that stands behind it.[11]

As suggested, a similar approach can be developed with regard to contemporary culture, including its most popular manifestations. In the present work the author has not undertaken this approach in the same systematic fashion as Prokofieff; rather, this collection of essays represents a looser endeavour in the same direction. As Prokofieff writes in his book, it is hoped similarly with this modest work that it 'may put the reader in the position of gradually developing a *judgement of his own* which will enable him to discern the *full*, and not only a partial, reality...'

Thought as a spiritual force

In his most concise definition of Anthroposophy, Rudolf Steiner stated that: 'Anthroposophy is a path of *knowledge*, to guide the spiritual in the human being to the spiritual in the universe.'[12] Respecting the spiritual potential of present-day humanity, Steiner repeatedly requested his readers and listeners to accept nothing on faith or authority; for he recognized the importance of personal knowledge and understanding in our time. However, according to his research, such understanding is not only significant to the individual human being but is also critical to the hierarchies of spiritual beings. Through the free deed of cultivating clear, true spiritual thoughts, the individual enables exalted spiritual forces to strengthen their connection with humanity. In this light, the 'third way' of approaching contemporary culture becomes more than a means to personal advancement, having significant consequences for human civilization and the process of evolution. If individuals aspire to understand the truth behind the manifestations of popular culture, their work in this regard will already have a powerful effect in counteracting its dangerous and degenerate aspects.

To comprehend such a notion it is necessary to have a concept of the spiritual power of thought. 'Thoughts,' said Rudolf Steiner, 'are just as much a force as the electric current that flows from one apparatus to another.'[13] In his most fundamental work on meditation he wrote that one of the requirements of esoteric training is that

> ...we win through to the conviction that thoughts and feelings are as important for the world as actions. We should recognize that when we hate our fellow human beings it is just as destructive as when we physically strike them. This brings us once more to the insight that anything we do for our own improvement benefits not just ourselves but also the world. The world benefits as much from pure feelings and thoughts as from good deeds.[14]

Lecturing on spiritual development, Rudolf Steiner related how a true thought works '...to make our spiritual world richer and more full of content—which is necessary if humanity is to make progress'.[15]

With the above in mind it is possible to approach an understanding of Rudolf Steiner's extraordinary statement to Asya Turgeniev that had there been twelve true anthroposophists in Russia in 1917, the Bolsheviks would never have come to power.[16] The significance of intense spiritual work is similarly made clear in Steiner's final spoken words to members of the Anthroposophical Society, where he proclaimed that if 'in the near future, in four times twelve human beings, the Michael thought becomes fully alive', the light of the Michael stream would be able to work in future amongst humanity.[17] Likewise, we can understand why Rudolf Steiner took the trouble to talk to audiences about the causes of the First World War and the work of certain adversary occult groups (for example, in his lectures published as *The Karma of Untruthfulness*). For, as he stated in many instances, if sufficient numbers of people are aware of, and understand with sufficient insight and clarity, the work and aims of such adversary groups and the forces behind them, then this already weakens and counteracts their malign operations. In essence, therefore, we should hold to the conviction that 'nothing is lost that is done spiritually',[18] and that spiritual work can have an immeasurable effect on outward events.

'Moral breathing' and the Manichaean path

To understand more fully how this 'third way' can enable us to take the first steps in transforming the materialistic culture of our time, a brief mention will be made to an esoteric practice which is called 'moral breathing'. For a fuller exposition of this and its relation to the Manichaean and the Rosicrucian paths, the reader is advised to study the chapter entitled 'The Nature of Forgiveness and the Sevenfold Manichaean Initiation' in Sergei O. Prokofieff's seminal book *The Occult Significance of Forgiveness*. Prokofieff describes how in the future humankind will be able to unfold the faculty of moral breathing through spiritually 'inhaling' evil and 'exhaling' good. Although such a process will only be fully possible in the future, when humanity will be given the task of the gradual overcoming of evil, small beginnings can already be made in our time. This is enabled '... by means of an inner activity of the soul, everywhere to seek the spirit in matter. Initially, this takes place on the plane of thought, through the results of anthroposophical spiritual research being assimilated. The consequence of this is that individuals who had formerly always "inhaled" the materialistic conceptions of modern civilization learn in ever-growing measure to "exhale" the spiritual thoughts of modern spiritual science into this civilization...'[19] This process can be related to the deeply-Christian Manichaean principle in that it contains within it the mystery of the transformation of evil into good.[20]

As Lona Truding says of the third-century spiritual leader Mani: '... whereas [St] Augustine beheld a good and an evil state of mankind, forever separated, Mani realized that those forces which are good need to be used for the transformation and the redemption of evil. The Manichaeans saw in the search for the evil itself the beginning of the transformation. This search was an act of cognition.'[21]

While it must be emphasized that the overcoming of evil in the fullest sense is only truly possible in the distant future (in the next, sixth, great period of earth evolution, 'which will witness the highest flowering and the widest diffusion on earth of the Manichaean Mysteries'),[22] nevertheless the approach to contemporary culture described above can be seen as a small beginning towards this 'moral breathing' of the future and the work of the Manichaean stream of transforming evil rather than seeking to push it away.

Finally, it should be mentioned that such work can only successfully be achieved through a genuine interest (rather than a morbid feeling of inner sacrifice) and, ultimately, a mood of love towards what is being considered. In this sense, one can think of Rudolf Steiner's immersion into the materialistic ideas of the scientist Ernst Haeckel or the anti-Christian philosopher Nietzsche. Both his books[23] on these individuals show an objective inner enthusiasm towards their ideas, even though they were contrary to his own. The starting point for each of the studies in this book has also been an *interest* (and sometimes a sympathy, which had then to be objectified) in the particular person or pheno-menon taken as a focus for study.

NOTES AND REFERENCES

Readers should note that Rudolf Steiner's books and lectures were originally published in German (Rudolf Steiner Verlag, Dornach, Switzerland). In the notes below, references have been given only to the English translations.

Chapter 1

First published in an earlier version in Das Goetheanum *(14 August and 16 October 1994), and* Anthroposophy Today *(Autumn 1994).*

1 *The Independent*, London, 29 July 1994.
2 Ibid.
3 *The Sunday Telegraph*, London, 14 February 1993.

Chapter 2

First published in an earlier version in Das Goetheanum *(2 April 1995), and* Anthroposophy Today *(Spring/Summer 1995).*

1 New York/London, MTV Books/Callaway/Boxtree, 1994.
2 Manfred Schmidt-Brabant, 'Anatomy of Violence Today', *Die Drei*, Stuttgart, May 1993.
3 *Die sociale Grundforderung unserer Zeit*, GA 186, Dornach, Rudolf Steiner Verlag.
4 *The Spiritual Origins of Eastern Europe and the Future Mysteries of the Holy Grail*, London, Temple Lodge Publishing, 1993, p. 272.
5 Ibid., p. 308.
6 Ibid., p. 314.
7 Ibid., p. 344.

Chapter 3

First published in an earlier version in Das Goetheanum *(19 November 1995), and* Anthroposophy Today *(Winter 1995).*

1 *Vox* magazine, London, January 1995.
2 Ibid.
3 *Moviewatch*, ITV, February 1995.
4 Ibid.
5 The Guide, *The Guardian*, London, 27 May 1995.
6 Ezekiel 25:17.
7 Lecture of 15 September 1912, *The Gospel of St Mark*, New York/London, Anthroposophic Press/Rudolf Steiner Press, 1986.
8 *The Guardian*, 19 November 1994.
9 *Vox*, op. cit.
10 *The Guardian*, 29 October 1994.
11 *Time Out*, London, 1 February 1994.
12 *The Portal of Initiation*, translated by Ruth and Hans Pusch, Toronto, Steiner Book Centre, 1973.
13 Ibid.
14 Ibid.
15 Ibid.
16 Ibid.
17 Ibid.
18 *The Guardian*, op. cit.
19 Lecture of 27 February 1917, *Cosmic and Human Metamorphoses*, London, Rudolf Steiner Publishing Co., 1926.
20 *Vox*, op. cit.
21 Ibid.
22 Ibid.
23 Ibid.
24 Ibid.
25 *The Guardian*, op. cit.
26 Quentin Tarantino, *Pulp Fiction* screenplay, London, Faber and Faber, 1994.
27 See, for example, the case of the child Jamie Bulger who was killed by two other young boys. The popular press claimed an (unproved) link with the horror film *Child's Play 3*.

28 *Time* (US edition), New York, 12 June 1995.
29 Lecture of 27 February 1917, op. cit.
30 Ibid.
31 *Time Out*, op. cit.
32 Ibid.
33 *Moving Pictures*, BB2, February 1995.
34 *Time Out*, op. cit.
35 Lecture of 27 February 1917, op. cit.
36 Letter in *Info 3*, Frankfurt, issue 4, 1983. For an in-depth analysis of cinema, see also the article 'Kino, Karma und Reinkarnation', Rudolf Bind and Martin Barkhoff, in *Das Goetheanum*, Dornach, 13 September 1987.

Chapter 4

1 *The Guardian*, London, 10 June 1995.
2 *Time* (US edition), New York, 12 June 1995.
3 *The Guardian*, op. cit.
4 For a penetrating history of rap see David Toop, *The Rap Attack: African Jive to New York Hip Hop*, London, Pluto Press, 1985; and S. H. Fernando, Jr., *The New Beats, Exploring the Music, Culture and Attitudes of Hip-Hop*, Edinburgh, Payback Press, 1995. Toop attempts to trace the roots of rap to the West African savannah Griots.
5 See, for example, Public Enemy, *It Takes a Nation of Millions to Hold Us Back* (Def Jam Recordings, 1988); The Jungle Brothers, *Done By the Forces of Nature* (Eternal, 1989); BDP, *Edutainment* (Jive, 1990); and Gang Starr, *Step in the Arena* (Cooltempo, 1991).
6 'Don't Believe the Hype', from *It Takes a Nation of Millions to Hold Us Back*, op. cit.
7 *The Source, The Magazine of Hip-Hop Music, Culture and Politics*, New York, October 1991.
8 *The Source*, December 1990.
9 *Melody Maker*, London, 26 November 1994.
10 *The New Beats*, op. cit, p. 101.
11 For a full treatment of this argument see previous chapter,

'Cinema, Violence and "Reality" in Art'. Rudolf Steiner once stated that: '... art can really be nothing else than a reflection of what human beings feel in relation to the universe. Of course this is possible at various levels and from various standpoints; but generally we can evaluate a work of art only when it expresses human feeling in such a way that through it the soul is opened to the secrets of the universe.' (Lecture of 6 October 1923, *The Four Seasons and the Archangels*, London, Rudolf Steiner Press, 1996.)

12 *The Source*, December 1990.
13 *The Source*, June 1994.
14 *The New Beats*, op. cit., p. 85.
15 *NME*, London, 25 November 1995.
16 'Jesse James', *The Diary* (Rap-a-Lot Records, 1994).
17 *The Source*, June 1994.
18 *The Source*, December 1990.
19 *Select*, London, April 1994.
20 Nathan McCall, 'My Rap Against Rap', *Reader's Digest*, May 1994.
21 Ibid.
22 *The Source*, October 1993.
23 Ibid.
24 *The Source*, June 94.
25 *The Source*, December 1990.
26 *NME*, London, 26 February 1994.
27 *Select*, April 1994.
28 *The Source*, December 1990.
29 *Time*, 12 June 1995.
30 Ibid.
31 *NME*, 3 December 1994.
32 *The Source*, June 1994.
33 *NME*, 6 August 1994.
34 *The Guardian*, 13 August 1994.
35 *Time*, 12 June 1995.
36 *The Face*, London, February 1994.
37 Sergei O. Prokofieff, *The Spiritual Origins of Eastern Europe and the Future Mysteries of the Holy Grail*, London, Temple Lodge Publishing, 1993, p. 285.
38 Ibid.

39 Ibid.
40 See Rudolf Steiner, *Towards Social Renewal*, London, Rudolf Steiner Press, 1977, and *The Renewal of the Social Organism*, New York/London, Anthroposophic Press/Rudolf Steiner Press, 1985.

Chapter 5

First published in an earlier version in Anthroposophy Today *(Summer 1992).*

Since the writing of this piece David Icke has become a leading figure within the New Age movement and has had several challenging books published.

1 *The Times*, London, 20 March 1991.
2 *The Sunday Times* magazine, London, 13 October 1991.
3 David Icke, *The Truth Vibrations*, Aquarian Press, London, 1991.
4 *The Sunday Times*, 31 March 1991.
5 *The Sun*, London, 28 March 1991.
6 *The Daily Mirror*, London, 28 March 1991.
7 Ibid., *The Sunday Times*, op. cit. 4.
8 *The Daily Mirror*, op. cit.
9 *The Sun*, op. cit.
10 *The Daily Mirror*, op. cit.
11 *The Truth Vibrations*, op. cit., p. 17.
12 Ibid., p. 32.
13 Ibid., p. 37.
14 *The Sunday Times* magazine, op. cit. 2.
15 *The Truth Vibrations*, op. cit., p. 86.
16 Ibid., p 74.
17 Los Angeles, Summit University Press, 1971.
18 See, for example, Rudolf Steiner's lecture of 9 April 1924, *Karmic Relationships*, Vol. VI, London, Rudolf Steiner Press, 1989.
19 See Rudolf Steiner's lecture of 27 September 1911, *Esoteric Christianity and the Mission of Christian Rosenkreutz*, London, Rudolf Steiner Press, 1984.

20 Ilona Schubert, *Reminiscences of Rudolf Steiner*, London, Temple Lodge Press, 1991.

21 See, for example, Rudolf Steiner's lecture of 27 November 1916, *The Karma of Vocation*, New York, Anthroposophic Press, 1984; and lectures of 17 and 18 October 1915, *The Occult Movement in the Nineteenth Century*, London, Rudolf Steiner Press, 1973.

22 Lecture of 17 October 1915, *The Occult Movement in the Nineteenth Century*, ibid.

23 *The Truth Vibrations*, op. cit., p. 119.

24 Ibid., pp. 27–29.

25 Ibid., p. 36.

26 Ibid., p. 137.

27 *The Guardian*, London, 6 January 1992.

28 *The Sunday Times* magazine, op. cit. 2.

29 Rudolf Steiner's lecture of 20 July 1924, *Karmic Relationships*, Vol. VI, London, Rudolf Steiner Press, 1989.

30 *The Truth Vibrations*, op. cit., p. 117.

31 Ibid., p. 116.

32 Lecture of 13 October 1911, *From Jesus to Christ*, London, Rudolf Steiner Press, 1973.

33 *The Truth Vibrations*, op. cit., pp. 10–11.

34 Ibid., p. 120.

35 Ibid., p. 109.

36 Lecture of 17 October 1915, *The Occult Movement in the Nineteenth Century*, op. cit.

37 Rudolf Steiner's notes about the Theosophical Society for Edouard Schuré (September 1907), reproduced in Rudolf Steiner and Marie Steiner von Sivers, *Correspondence and Documents 1901–1925*, London, Rudolf Steiner Press, 1988. For a deeper study of this question, see Sergei O. Prokofieff, *The East in the Light of the West, Two Eastern Streams of the Twentieth Century in the Light of Christian Esotericism, Part 1: Agni Yoga*, London, Temple Lodge Publishing, 1993.

38 Ibid.

39 *The Truth Vibrations*, p. 23.

40 Ibid., p. 142.

41 Ibid., p. 140.

Chapter 6

First published in an earlier version in Anthroposophy Today *(Autumn 1993 and Spring 1994) and* Das Goetheanum *(30 January 1994).*

1 *The Times*, London, 19 March 1991.
2 According to statistics published in an article entitled 'Second Class from Cradle to Grave' (*The Times*, London, 17 October 1995), recent research shows that a third of North American blacks are born into poverty, with two-thirds raised by single mothers; only 12 per cent receive university degrees (compared to 23 per cent of whites); a third of black males in their twenties are in prison, on parole or on probation; black men are eight times more likely to be murdered than white men; black unemployment is twice the rate of whites; and life expectancy for blacks is 69.6 years compared to 76.5 years for whites.
3 *Late Show* special, 'From the Pyramids to the Projects', BBC2, 1990.
4 Ibid.
5 For further analysis and a history of rap see Chapter 4, 'Gangsta Rap, Reality and "Supermaterialism"'.
6 Ice Cube, 'When Will They Shoot?' from *The Predator*, Priority Records, 1992.
7 Ibid., 'Now I Gotta Wet 'Cha'.
8 Da Lench Mob, 'Buck Tha Devil' from *Guerillas in tha Mist*, East West Records, 1992.
9 NWA, 'Sa Prize (Part 2)' from *100 Miles And Runnin'*, Priority Records, 1990.
10 *The Autobiography of Malcolm X*, with the assistance of Alex Haley, Harmondsworth, Penguin Books, 1968. The following account of Malcolm X's life is based on his own account, and Thulani Davis, *Malcolm X*, New York, Stewart, Tabori & Chang, 1993. For a more critical account, see also Bruce Perry, *Malcolm, The Life of a Man Who Changed Black America*, New York, Station Hill, 1993.
11 Elijah Muhammad, *Message to the Blackman in America*, Chicago, Muhammad's Temple No. 2, 1965.

12 *The Autobiography of Malcolm X*, op. cit., p. 256. For confirmation of Elijah Muhammad's teachings see also his *Message to the Blackman in America*, op. cit.
13 *The Autobiography of Malcolm X*, op. cit.
14 Ibid., p. 257.
15 Ibid., p. 306.
16 Ibid.
17 Ibid.
18 *Message to the Blackman in America*, op. cit., p. 17.
19 *The Autobiography of Malcolm X*, op. cit., pp. 267–77.
20 'The Muslim Programme', reproduced in *Message to the Blackman in America*, op. cit.
21 *The Autobiography of Malcolm X*, op. cit., p. 348.
22 Ibid., p. 443.
23 Ibid., p. 452.
24 Ibid., p. 454.
25 Ibid., p. 479.
26 Ibid., p. 480.
27 Ibid., p. 483.
28 Ibid., p. 321.
29 Ibid., p. 489.
30 Ibid., Alex Haley's Foreword, p. 57.
31 Ibid., p. 62.
32 Ibid., p. 44.
33 Ibid., p. 48.
34 Ibid., p. 53.
35 Rudolf Steiner's lecture of 17 February 1918, *The Mission of the Archangel Michael*, New York, Anthroposophic Press, 1961.
36 Ibid.
37 *The Autobiography of Malcolm X*, op. cit., p. 73.
38 *Message to the Blackman in America*, op. cit, p. 23.
39 Ibid., p. 32.
40 Ibid., p. 24.
41 Ibid., p. 31.
42 Ibid., the chapter entitled 'The Devil' (pp.110–22) where the whole 'creation story' of the white race is described.
43 Ibid., p. 291.
44 Ibid., p. 304.
45 Ibid., p. 6.

46 Ibid., p. 9.

47 Ibid., p. 26.

48 Ibid., p. 18.

49 Elijah Muhammad's teaching is still influential today, particularly in the rap music scene. For example, on their recording 'Ain't no Mystery' (from *In God We Trust*, Elektra Records, 1992), the group Brand Nubian pose the question: 'Can you tell me where to find that mystery God? I don't see him... / I've searched and searched but there's still no sign...' Their answer is: 'It's got to be a trick for the deaf, dumb and blind / ... the black man is God, it ain't no mystery.' Another follower of the Nation of Islam, Lakim Shabazz, asserts: '... I'm God, I've got the truth, the proof...' ('Black is Back', from *Pure Righteousness*, BCM Records, 1989).

50 See Nicholas Goodrick-Clarke, *The Occult Roots of Nazism*, Wellingborough, Aquarian Press, 1985. For an anthroposophical perspective see Sergei O. Prokofieff, *The Spiritual Origins of Eastern Europe and the Future Mysteries of the Holy Grail*, London, Temple Lodge Publishing, 1993, note 131 of Part Three, pp. 510–12.

51 Rudolf Steiner, lecture of 11 April 1912: 'Address given to the Russian members of the Theosophical Society', London, Rudolf Steiner House Library (Typescript Z409).

52 Ibid.

53 A tangible example of such a 'revenge'—in the form of an eastern-inspired teaching which seeks to replace the central position of Christ in Earth evolution—is presented in Sergei O. Prokofieff's book *The East in the Light of the West, Two Eastern Streams in the Light of Christian Esotericism, Part 1: Agni Yoga*, London, Temple Lodge Publishing, 1993.

54 H. P. Blavatsky, *From the Caves and Jungles of Hindustan*, Wheaton, Theosophical Publishing House, 1975, p. xxxv.

55 Ibid., p. 49.

56 Quoted from *The East in the Light of the West*, op. cit., p. 108 (translated from Blavatsky's original Russian). In *From the Caves and Jungles of Hindostan* (op. cit., p. 462) this phrase is rendered into English more demurely as 'the hated and despised white race'.

57 Ibid.

58 For the connection of certain eastern occultists with 'occult materialism' see Sergei O. Prokofieff, *The East in the Light of the West*, op. cit.

59 *Malcolm, The Life of a Man Who Changed Black America*, op. cit.

60 *Message to the Blackman in America*, op. cit., p. 20.

61 K. Paul Johnson, *The Masters Revealed, Madame Blavatsky and the Myth of the Great White Lodge*, Albany, State University of New York Press, 1994.

62 Of course, none of what has been said is intended to detract from the fact that millions of people of African origin suffered, many to their deaths, as a consequence of the slave trade and its aftermath. It is the exploitation of such suffering by occult groups which is the concern here.

Chapter 7

First published in an earlier version in Anthroposophy Today *(Spring 1994).*

1 Rudolf Steiner, lecture of 15 November 1917, *Geographic Medicine and the Secret of the Double*, New York, Mercury Press, 1986.

2 For a complete picture of cosmic evolution from the Old Saturn period see Rudolf Steiner's book *Occult Science, An Outline*, London, Rudolf Steiner Press, 1962.

3 For a full description see Rudolf Steiner's lecture of 10 June 1910, *The Mission of the Individual Folk Souls*, London, Rudolf Steiner Press, 1970.

4 From Rudolf Steiner's various statements on the subject of the original races we can list seven main types: African, Caucasian, Mongolian, Malayan, Red Indian, Semitic and Turanian.

5 Rudolf Steiner, lecture of 10 June 1910, *The Mission of the Individual Folk Souls*, op. cit.

6 Rudolf Steiner, lecture of 20 June 1908, *The Apocalypse of St John*, London, Anthroposophical Publishing Company, 1958.

7 Rudolf Steiner, lecture of 16 August 1908, *Universe Earth and Man*, London: Rudolf Steiner Publishing Company, 1955.

8 Rudolf Steiner, lecture of 1 June 1908, *The Influence of Spiritual Beings Upon Man*, New York, Anthroposophic Press, 1961.

9 Ibid.

10 *Universe Earth and Man*, op. cit., lecture VI.

11 Ibid., lecture VIII.

12 St Paul expressed this connection of the ego with Christ with the words: 'it is no longer I who live, but Christ who lives in me' (Galations 3:20).

13 Rudolf Steiner, lecture of 9 January 1916, 'The Spiritual Unity of Mankind through the Christ-impulse', *Anthroposophical Quarterly*, London, Anthroposophical Society in Great Britain, Spring 1968.

14 Ibid.

15 Ibid.

16 Rudolf Steiner, lecture of 1 June 1908, *The Influence of Spiritual Beings Upon Man*, op. cit.

17 Ibid.

18 *Universe Earth and Man*, op. cit., lecture XI.

19 Rudolf Steiner, lecture of 16 November 1917, *Geographic Medicine and the Secret of the Double*, op. cit.

20 Ibid.

21 Rudolf Steiner, lecture of 19 November 1917, *The Reappearance of Christ in the Etheric*, New York/London, Anthroposophic Press/Rudolf Steiner Press, 1983.

22 This is confirmed in a wonderful way in the so-called 'Dreamtime' memories of the Australian Aborigines.

23 Rudolf Steiner, lecture of 25 October 1906, *The Occult Significance of Blood*, London, Rudolf Steiner Press, 1967.

24 Rudolf Steiner, lecture of 31 October 1920, *The New Spirituality and the Christ Experience of the Twentieth Century*, London/New York, Rudolf Steiner Press/Anthroposophic Press, 1988.

25 Rudolf Steiner, lecture of 7 January 1917, *The Karma of Untruthfulness*, Vol. II, London, Rudolf Steiner Press, 1992.

26 Ibid., lecture of 6 January 1917.

27 *The Mission of the Individual Folk Souls*, op. cit., lecture of 9 June 1910.

28 Ibid., lecture of 10 June 1910.

29 Ibid., lecture of 9 June 1910.

30 *The New Spirituality and the Christ Experience of the Twentieth Century*, op. cit., lecture of 31 October 1920.

31 *The Karma of Untruthfulness*, Vol. II, op. cit., lecture of 6 January 1917.

32 *The Mission of the Individual Folk Souls*, op. cit., lecture of 7 June 1910.

33 Rudolf Steiner, lecture of 17 February 1918, *The Mission of the Archangel Michael*, New York, Anthroposophic Press, 1961.

34 *The New Spirituality and the Christ Experience of the Twentieth Century*, op. cit., lecture of 31 October 1920.

35 Ibid., lecture of 31 October 1920.

36 Ita Wegman, 'To all Members', 24 May 1925, *Esoteric Studies, The Michael Impulse*, London, Temple Lodge Publishing, 1993.

37 *Geographic Medicine and the Mystery of the Double*, op. cit., lecture of 16 November 1917.

38 *The Mission of the Individual Folk Souls*, op. cit., lecture 17 June 1910.

Appendix

1 *Knowledge of the Higher Worlds, How is it Achieved*, London, Rudolf Steiner Press, also available as *How to Know Higher Worlds*, New York, Anthroposophic Press; *Theosophy*, Anthroposophic Press; *Occult Science, An Outline*, Rudolf Steiner Press; *The Philosophy of Freedom*, Rudolf Steiner Press, also available as *Intuitive Thinking as a Spiritual Path*, Anthroposophic Press.

2 It should be pointed out, however, that in his fundamental works Rudolf Steiner repeatedly conveyed to his readers that they could judge the material with their ordinary faculty of unprejudiced thought. For example, in the Preface to *Occult Science* he states: 'Although the book concerns researches beyond the reach of the sense-bound intellect, nothing is here presented which cannot be grasped with open-minded thought and with the healthy feeling for the truth possessed by everyone who will apply these gifts of human nature.' (London, Rudolf Steiner Press, 1963, p. 24.)

3 See note 1.

4 *How to Know Higher Worlds*, op. cit., p. 77.

5 Lecture of 21 September 1923, *Eine Erinnerung an die Grund-*

steinfeier zur Befestigung des anthroposophischen Wesens, Dornach, private printing, 1942.

6 See 'The Lies that Made the Gulf War', *The Guardian*, London, 16 December 1995. Her film *Riding the Storm: How to Tell Lies and Win Wars* was shown on Channel 4 television on 3 January 1996.

7 Ibid., *The Guardian*.

8 Ibid.

9 See for example *The Karma of Untruthfulness*, Vols. 1 and 2, London, Rudolf Steiner Press, 1988 and 1992; *From Symptom to Reality in Modern History*, Rudolf Steiner Press, 1976; and *The Fall of the Spirits of Darkness*, Rudolf Steiner Press, 1994.

10 London, Temple Lodge Publishing, 1993.

11 Ibid., pp. 2–3.

12 *Anthroposophical Leading Thoughts*, London, Rudolf Steiner Press, 1973.

13 *Brotherhood and the Struggle for Existence*, Spring Valley, Mercury Press, 1980, p. 12.

14 *How to Know Higher Worlds*, op. cit., p. 100.

15 *Theosophy of the Rosicrucian*, London, Rudolf Steiner Press, 1966, p. 61.

16 *The Spiritual Origins of Eastern Europe*, op. cit., p. 471.

17 *The Last Address*, London, Rudolf Steiner Press, 1967, p. 18.

18 *Brotherhood and the Struggle for Existence*, op. cit., p. 13.

19 *The Occult Significance of Forgiveness*, 3rd edition, London, Temple Lodge Publishing, 1995, p. 124.

20 Of course, it is not in any way being suggested that outer practical work is not important. On the contrary, as Prokofieff shows, Manichaeanism seeks to bring thinking into the will, leading to the 'renewal of practically all realms of human life and activity—art, science (Goetheanism), education, agriculture, medicine, banking, the social order, and so on...' (*The Occult Significance of Forgiveness*, op. cit. p. 124.)

21 *A Miracle for Our Time*, London, Temple Lodge Publishing, 1994, p. 24.

22 *The Occult Significance of Forgiveness*, op. cit., p. 120.

23 See 'Haeckel and His Opponents' in *Three Essays on Haeckel and Karma*, London, Theosophical Publishing Society, 1914, and *Friedrich Nietzsche, Fighter for Freedom*, New Jersey, Rudolf Steiner Publications, 1960.